Alice Neville, is a freelance writer whose books include biographies of Louis XIV (1983) and Nelson and is currently membership secretary of the National Art Collections Fund. She was the founder of The Open Door – a self-help organization for agoraphobes – which she started in 1965 and ran for 10 years. Together with her husband she set up an alcoholics counselling service. She is married to a solicitor and they have four grown up children.

Also published by Century Arrow

The Bristol Diet *Dr Alec Forbes*
Curing PMT *Moira Carpenter*
How to Beat Fatigue *Louis Proto*

'*Aggie Phobie*'

Who's Afraid of Agoraphobia?

Facing up to fear and anxiety
a self-help guide

Alice Neville

Illustrated by Keith Addey

Century Arrow
London Melbourne Auckland Johannesburg

A Century Arrow Book
Published by Arrow Books Limited
Brookmount House, 62–65 Chandos Place, Covent Garden,
London WC2N 4NW

An imprint of Century Hutchinson Ltd
London   Melbourne   Sydney   Auckland
Johannesburg and agencies throughout
the world

First published 1986
Century Arrow edition

This book is sold subject to the condition that it shall
not, by way of trade or otherwise, be lent, resold, hired
out, or otherwise circulated without the publisher's prior
consent in any form of binding or cover other than that in
which it is published and without a similar condition
including this condition being imposed on the subsequent
purchaser

Copyright © Alice Neville 1986
Illustrations © Keith Addey 1986

Set in 11/12 pt Linotron Sabon by
Rowland Phototypesetting Ltd,
Bury St Edmunds, Suffolk
Printed and bound in Great Britain by
The Guernsey Press Co. Ltd, Guernsey, Channel Islands

British Library Cataloguing in Publication Data
Neville, Alice
Who's afraid of agoraphobia?
1. Agoraphobia
Rn: Patricia A. Holmes   I. Title
616.85′225   RC535

ISBN 0 09 946630 9

To 'Min', my mother, who talked me out of innumerable
telephone boxes

Acknowledgements

My grateful thanks are due to the following authors who have given me permission to quote passages from their books: Jane Madders, Professor Isaac M. Marks, Dr Ross Mitchell, Ruth Hurst Vose, Dr Garth Wood and Tuula Tuornaa.

I would also like to thank Peter Blythe of the Institute for Neuro-Physiological Psychology and Marie Ljunggren for their help and advice with the chapter on organic brain dysfunction.

Greetings and special thanks go to all past members of The Open Door from whose letters I have acquired much of what I know about agoraphobia, and to Keith Addey whose cartoons help to create the light-hearted approach I have used throughout the book.

Contents

Introduction

Does your heart beat faster when you shop in a supermarket? Do your legs turn to jelly and does your mouth go
dry if you have to travel on a bus or train? Do feelings of
sheer panic strike suddenly and threaten to overwhelm you
for no apparent reason? Everyone experiences these unpleasant symptoms from time to time and the majority of
people can shrug them off, reasoning that they were physically unwell or under some stress on that particular occasion. However, when these frightening sensations persist
and the sufferer is in a constant state of anxiety, trying to
avoid the situations where panic strikes time and time again
until their whole life is affected and living in fear becomes a
permanent condition – this is agoraphobia.

Those who have not experienced this frightening problem
naturally find it difficult to comprehend the extent of the
suffering it causes. It is a condition that defies easy description, for the word *agoraphobia* is used as a collective term
for a number of unpleasant sensations which can, if
allowed, wreck the life of the sufferer but which appear to
bear little relation to the accepted definition: a fear of open
spaces. Fear is there certainly, but fear of what? Not of the
great outdoors, the shopping centre, the motorway – but
fear of the terrifying irrational feeling of anxiety escalating
to panic which for no apparent reason can overwhelm the

agoraphobic person. One person may well experience these feelings in a shopping centre, another in an open field, another on a bus or in church. Yet another sufferer may be affected in each one of these situations, but what we have to understand is that it is not the church nor the supermarket that is the object of the phobia – these are just places to be avoided because they are the settings associated with the frightening sensations.

Having to cope with such feelings is bad enough, but those who suffer from agoraphobia feel that they are consequently isolated from the 'normal' world because they cannot explain exactly what is wrong, why they are trying to avoid certain situations and only feel at ease in their home surroundings. Relatives, friends and colleagues – even their own doctor – frequently turn out to be less than understanding. After all, it is easy to be sympathetic when someone close to you is ill or in distress, but after weeks and months of persistent 'unwellness' for no apparent reason, tempers become short, patience wears thin and the unfortunate recommendation to 'pull yourself together' is directed at the poor agoraphobe whose fervent wish is to be able to do just that!

Busy GPs hand out tranquillizers and a few encouraging words if the patient is lucky; perhaps a brisk assurance that 'everybody feels like this from time to time'. When the problem persists, psychiatric help may be sought, but too often this just means more pills. Which is not to say that specialist treatment is not available; in fact there are many psychiatrists and hospitals providing a programme of therapy for agoraphobes, but these are spread thinly throughout the country and the unlucky patient often finds that there is no help available in her particular area. Since travelling any distance from home may be one of the major problems, specialist treatment may well be way out of reach.

This book considers how agoraphobia is treated, the various types of therapy available and the extent to which they are proving successful. We shall also consider some of the more unconventional approaches to the problem and, most important, study ways in which the agoraphobe can help herself, because in the long run most of the hard work must be done by the sufferer once she understands how to tackle the problem.

Every agoraphobe suffers from an over-active imagination. Her days are spent anticipating the problems which must be faced – what might happen if she finds herself in a phobic situation. She imagines how she will feel if she does have to face such a situation and is horrified to find that merely thinking about the symptoms may cause them to materialize in the safety of her own home.

Avoiding the situations in which she feels panicky or ill at ease causes the agoraphobe to retreat until she may in extreme cases become completely housebound. Note the phrase *in extreme cases*; the majority of agoraphobes do *not* become permanently housebound. Too many articles in the press, interviews on radio and television are inclined to overstate the 'housebound housewife' syndrome and the picture is often presented of a tragic figure imprisoned in her home with little hope of ever leading a normal life, suggesting that this is a typical agoraphobia sufferer and frightening the life out of hundreds of others who immediately assume that this is their inevitable fate.

Many, many people suffering from agoraphobia lead completely normal lives – travelling to work each day, coping with shopping and social functions, going on holiday. Certainly they are under a good deal of stress and living with their phobia may mean that the quality of their lives is affected to some degree, but they keep going in the hope that one day things will improve.

The number of agoraphobes in Britain is estimated to be

half a million, but this figure is based on the number of people seeking treatment for the condition.

In the USA and Canada recent statistics show that 10 people in every 1,000 can expect to have agoraphobic symptoms ranging from totally disabling to mildly disturbing; applying this to the United Kingdom would indicate that the actual figure in this country is around three million.

One of the reasons why the agoraphobe is often disinclined to seek treatment is that she finds it so difficult to describe her feelings and fears that she may be labelled mentally ill. So, when a fellow sufferer is persuaded to talk about her problem to a sympathetic interviewer on television or in a magazine, letters and phone calls flood in to say, 'Thank God, at last somebody understands how I feel!'

As a result of a magazine article describing my own experiences while suffering from agoraphobia I started a self-help organization called The Open Door; during the ten years I was associated with TOD, I was in contact with over 30,000 agoraphobics. This book is based upon my personal experiences and those of my TOD contacts. Case histories quoted are from the original newsletters and more recent personal contacts unless otherwise stated.

Because the majority of agoraphobes are women and because I am drawing on my own experiences, viewing the problems from a woman's angle, I refer to the agoraphobe throughout the book as 'she'. I hope that the male sufferers will forgive me for this and assure them that they have not been ignored.

Having a fairly good understanding of the agoraphobic temperament, I know that many people avoid reading the helpful books which have been written about their condition: they may be frightened to find out if their symptoms point to some serious mental illness; wondering if they will add to their own list of odd feelings by reading about others;

fearful they may learn that there is no hope of recovery. This book is meant to reassure – there is no doom-laden message, so keep reading!

CHAPTER 1

What is Agoraphobia?

'Oh what can ail thee, knight at arms? . . .'

Keats

The Greeks had a word for it; *agora*, the place of assembly, and *phobos*, terror or flight, though the term agoraphobia was not used until the late nineteenth century when a German psychiatrist named Westphal described: 'the impossibility of walking through certain streets or squares, or possibility of so doing only with resultant dread of anxiety'.

Phobos – terror or flight. Flight is the key word; when panic strikes, the overwhelming need is to escape. If you are out in the open you must get under cover; if you are in a confined space you look around wildly for an exit . . . must get away from the people milling round you; must escape from the noise, the silence, the bright lights, the darkness. So many things to dread and each of them so different; no wonder the sufferer is confused to be told that agoraphobia is the problem when she feels just as panic-stricken in a lift or hemmed in by a crowd of people – isn't this *claustrophobia*?

The definitions of the two states may appear to be contradictory, but agoraphobia and claustrophobia both apply to a state of anxiety which manifests itself in certain situations, causing feelings of panic and a need to escape from and

*The Greeks had
a word for it*

avoid these situations. *Trapped!* Inside or out the feelings
are the same.

Thousands of people who would call themselves normal
and well-balanced, otherwise untroubled by any nervous
problem, will freely admit to sensations of mild claustrophobia in certain situations. For some reason this is quite
OK; claustrophobia is a socially acceptable problem as it
does not have a devastating effect on the sufferer's lifestyle
and is accepted with tolerance, even sympathy, by the
majority of people who can identify with it and who will
suggest the obvious solution – avoid the situation.

> I walk up four flights of stairs to my office each day. I tell myself
> that the exercise is good for me, but really there is no way I am
> going to use the lift. On the occasions I have forced myself to do
> so, I have felt physically ill and am terrified I might faint.
>
> Jan (20) secretary.

> I avoid travelling by Underground, though it is time-consuming getting around the city by bus. The whole atmosphere of an underground station induces feelings of acute panic ... the lighting, the hum of the air conditioning and the horrible rattle of the trains echoing through the tunnel. If I actually got into one of those awful things, I'm sure I would have to be carried out feet first.
>
> Betty (mid-30s) married.

Almost everyone at some time feels sick, weak, faint or over-anxious, but these feelings are soon shaken off and quickly forgotten once we have assured ourselves that there was a reason – we were one degree under at the time, recovering from 'flu, an operation, a nasty shock or even just a hangover.

However, the agoraphobe experiences these sensations over and over again until, upset and worried silly because she cannot understand *why* she feels this way, she begins to avoid the dreaded situations and her nervous system becomes so sensitized that even thinking about them can trigger off a full-scale panic attack. Now she is faced with the most crippling phobia of them all: fear of fear itself.

Though sufferers have often been unwilling to admit to being agoraphobic, the condition has been recognized for a long time. Richard Burton wrote in 1621 of:

> one that durst not walk alone from home for fear he should swoon or die ... if he be in a throng, middle of a church or multitude, where he may not well go out, though he sit at ease he is so misaffected.

Florence Nightingale in later life, with no physical outlet for her tremendous nervous energy, became housebound and was a semi-invalid for many years. After the shock of Prince Albert's death, Queen Victoria retreated from public life, unable to face her subjects *en masse*. For most of her youth

Elizabeth Barrett was confined to her couch with physical symptoms which miraculously disappeared after Robert Browning whisked her off to Italy and married her. Even in fiction there is Charles Dickens' Miss Havisham in *Great Expectations*, housebound since being jilted on her wedding day.

Shock, anxiety, emotional and physical frustration often lie behind the development of agoraphobia symptoms. How many swooning Victorian matrons languishing on their day-beds, how many wilting maidens in a fit of 'vapours' or slipping into a decline might be recognized as agoraphobic today?

By the 1920s it was accepted that many women were suffering from 'nervous debility' brought on by the stresses and strains of the era, though it was assumed that the 'lower classes' did not suffer from these problems, lacking the refinement and delicate sensibilities of the middle-class housewife who for the first time was having to cope without cook, housemaid, nanny, dressmaker and other servants. The magazines of the time are full of letters from ladies suffering from shattered nerves who could no longer withdraw into a state of genteel ill-health, but had to run their households and look after their families single-handed:

> I wake each morning with this dark cloud hanging over me as I wonder how I will be able to cope with my household duties. Visiting my friends used to be a pleasurable activity but I now begin to dread having to leave the house. If I have to walk any distance I find myself becoming breathless and agitated. My heart pounds and my vision seems distorted. I am assured by my doctor that I am suffering 'merely' from a nervous disorder but I fear that if it gets a grip I may eventually become a nervous invalid.
>
> Letter to *Woman* magazine.

Rest and quiet, wholesome food and at least ten hours' sleep each night, advised the agony aunts of the twenties, suggesting that ladies should avoid overtaxing their nervous systems and lead a tranquil life; this involved refraining from listening overmuch to the wireless or calling on the brain to deal with too great a variety of subjects in quick succession.

'Life is moving too fast for many of us,' wrote Flora Klixman, editor of *Woman*. 'We are all having to cope with the pace of modern living.' As an afterthought she suggested that a long sea voyage might be beneficial for over-stimulated constitutions:

> Household cares have gone for the time being; She (the mistress of the home) need do nothing but rest in a deck-chair with her feet up, reading, doing fancy work, or sleeping (which is of priceless worth to the nervous woman) and health and strength accumulates mysteriously.

Agoraphobia became known as the 'housebound house-wife's syndrome' and the sufferer had to cope with the condition as best she could, often taking on the role of nervous invalid or martyr to ill-health with some vaguely defined 'heart' condition. Anything was better than admitting to symptoms which might be regarded as the onset of serious mental illness.

How distressing it is to suffer from a complaint which has no obvious physical symptoms; how easy to be labelled a malingerer. Agoraphobes have been known to claim that they would sooner break a limb than suffer from a nervous disorder, as plaster cast or crutches would invoke a concerned and sympathetic response rather than a cynical disbelief that someone outwardly healthy could be experiencing such torment.

Because I look all right, none of the staff at school believe me when I say I feel really ill. I honestly think there is something terribly wrong with me, but I'm told to pull myself together. I know I take too many days off, but the school doctor fell about laughing when I suggested it might be my nerves making me feel bad. 'Nerves are often used as an excuse for avoiding something you don't want to do,' she said, and told me not to read medical bits in magazines as my imagination was out of control. I don't talk about it any more as no one understands; my friends would think I was very odd if I tried to explain how I felt and even my mother, who does try and understand, just says it's something I'll grow out of.

Jenny (15) schoolgirl.

Those who suffer from agoraphobia are inclined to think that they are unique; no one has ever experienced these frightening sensations before; nobody can possibly imagine how much they are suffering. So what *are* these strange and frightening feelings which the agoraphobic experiences?

Do not skip the following!
Many people cannot bear to read descriptions of symptoms – but you do not 'catch' feelings you read about, even if your imagination makes you feel uncomfortable. Keep reading and you will be surprised at your relief on knowing that you are not alone or different from everyone else.

Anxiety causes breathlessness, racing heart, nausea, dry mouth, clammy hands, over-breathing (hyperventilation), dizziness, a 'tight band' sensation round the head, vision disturbance, lump in the throat, buzzing or ringing in the ears. These are just some of the sensations that may be experienced, but every agoraphobic person can add to the list.

The feelings build up until they seem unbearable and the sufferer, clinging to the nearest static object to support her 'jelly legs', thinks, 'I can't stand it; my system won't take any more; I'll have a heart attack, a stroke, a brainstorm. I'll drop down dead, I know I will – at the very least I shall faint.' Unless you have always been a fainter, you *won't*! In the last century women swooned frequently in order to escape from situations they could not face up to, but it is very rare for an agoraphobe to employ this means of escape. The nervous 'collapse' is usually a conscious act that gets one out of a situation quickly as onlookers will rally round and provide sympathetic help:

> I sat on the pavement heaving and gasping for breath. I felt sick and dizzy; certain I was having some sort of fit or heart attack. I was conscious of a number of people hovering round me offering advice, and though I hate making an exhibition of myself in public, at that moment I couldn't have cared less. An ambulance arrived and I was whisked off to hospital where to my intense relief and even more intense embarrassment the symptoms immediately disappeared. The episode was diagnosed as an acute anxiety attack . . . I was never so mortified in my whole life.
>
> Marion (26) housewife with one child.

Most agoraphobes shrink at the thought of drawing attention to themselves and feel it is desperately important not to lose control, even though the inner struggle to appear calm increases the tension and panic as they fight to conceal their distress.

So what happens when the dreaded climax of a panic attack is reached? Nothing! The sensations can only reach a certain level and then they subside. This does not mean that there are no after-effects of such an experience; a severe attack can leave you in a highly sensitized state, weak and exhausted – but it cannot damage you physically.

One of the most terrifying feelings experienced during an attack of panic is that of depersonalization or unreality. This is a truly nightmarish sensation of being alone in an alien world where nothing seems real. Sounds echo seemingly from far away, your eyes play tricks as buildings appear to wobble and lean towards you. You feel as though you are hovering serveral inches above the ground; if you were hit by a bus you would not even feel it, because nothing is real. Your mind goes blank, your memory plays tricks. Who are you? Where are you? If only something would break the spell and return you to normality!

The agoraphobe's dilemma is that if she experiences these feelings in certain places, she will avoid these places in order to avert the panic; but with sensations of anxiety always present, she then begins to worry about other situations. She expects the panic to occur – so it does, almost as though her mind has an 'on' switch which operates whenever she thinks about the dreaded spot. The trouble is that she does not know how to operate the 'off' switch, so she retreats to safety – only soon nowhere is safe. If she is really unlucky, she will feel that the only place to avoid panic is behind her own front door; but even then, if the habit of switching on fear has become established, the security of her own home may not protect her from the dreaded attacks.

'Is this the end?' you may ask. Not so. There is a way out for nearly everyone. Contrary to the popular image, only a small percentage of agoraphobes become permanently housebound and a high proportion of these are people who have some disorder or personality problem which prevents them from tackling their fears and living a normal life. However, never forget that many of the housebound group became prisoners years and years ago before any real help was forthcoming or the problem properly understood. So if you read of someone who has been 'a prisoner in her home' for fifty years, don't despair. Probably it was not because the condition was incurable, but because the sufferer did not know how to break the habit of fear.

A situation from which there is no immediate escape

The other fears

In her overstrung nervous state the agoraphobic person finds that fears can multiply – fears which do not appear to come under the blanket term of agoraphobia but which are linked with the need for flight; the urge to get away from a particular situation. Fears about hospitals, doctors' and dentists' surgeries are understandable and shared by many non-phobic people who find these places anxiety provoking, but many agoraphobes cannot take a bath or shower, cannot visit a hairdresser, cannot sit at a table at meal-times or even talk on the telephone. A party, restaurant, church or classroom can be danger areas; any room full of people – even a one-to-one conversation with another person – can be the cause of build-up of anxiety because of the sensation of being trapped.

Sunday dinner at my in-laws' house was a nightmare, as the feelings started to build up even before we sat down at the table. I would feel sick and dizzy at the thought of having to sit still until the end of the meal – after all, there are only a few excuses one can have to leave the table . . . The family began to think I was anorexic because I just could not eat when I felt so trapped, but eventually I managed to explain to my mother-in-law how I felt and the whole situation was resolved. When I knew I could leave the room for a few moments whenever I needed to do so, the anxiety just subsided. I think my family were even more relieved than I was!

Margaret (24) married.

Many agoraphobes are free of symptoms when in a car, because the family car feels like an extension of the home; like a snail or a tortoise, these sufferers would like to carry

Her car is an extension of her home

with them a permanent shell into which they could retreat at any time.

The majority of sufferers can pinpoint the onset of agoraphobia whether it developed over a period of years or suddenly struck out of the blue. An accident, operation or childbirth; an emotional shock, bereavement, a prolonged period of stress – all these can lead to a sensitized nervous state which in certain individuals will ultimately develop into agoraphobia. Eventually the original cause ceases to matter; the agoraphobic person becomes trapped not by earlier traumas, stresses or strains but by sheer habit. She has so conditioned herself to feeling bad in certain situations that the outcome is inevitable if she happens to find herself thus 'trapped'. So what happens? She avoids them at all costs. Some long-term agoraphobics may not even be able to recall the last time they experienced a full-blown panic attack, but – trapped by the *fear* of fear – they are not prepared to risk facing a dreaded situation, 'just in case'.

CHAPTER 2

Through The Open Door

'Just at this moment Alice felt a very curious sensation . . .'
Lewis Carroll, *Alice in Wonderland*

Some years ago, I wrote an article about agoraphobia in which I described the feelings of a young woman as she pushed a pram along a busy street, talking to her two young children while fighting to keep at bay the feelings of panic which threatened to overcome her. Reciting a nursery rhyme, pointing to a frisky puppy pulling on its lead, stopping to look at toys in a shop window – all the while the mother seemed intent on capturing the children's interest, but in reality her main concern was to keep herself calm by concentrating on them, pushing down the urge to give in to panic and run for home as quickly as she could.

When this article appeared in a woman's magazine, it produced a flood of correspondence from agoraphobia sufferers throughout the country who felt that they could identify with the young mother, and expressed their relief in realizing that someone actually understood how they felt and had described the weird, frightening symptoms of the condition. Many who wrote had no idea what was wrong with them, and in some cases had not even realized that their problem actually had a name. At that time agoraphobia was a subject which had not been brought out into the open and discussed in the media, but now these people could collect their symptoms under a specific heading, while the mere fact of knowing that others were suffering in the same way helped them to face up to things and learn how to cope.

I do not know what prompted me to write about agoraphobia at that time. It had been many years since I had had any symptoms myself and I was now happily married with three young children, working part-time and enjoying a full social life — a very different person from the unhappy adolescent who had been convinced she would never be normal but would go through life a nervous wreck.

It started when I was seven years old. I was enjoying my weekly dancing class when someone switched on a light and I was immediately engulfed in what I could only describe to the adults present as a 'funny feeling'. It was not panic but a nightmare sensation of unreality and I was bewildered rather than frightened. The grown-ups decided that I was suffering from a nervous reaction to a recent tonsils operation, but even so they did not realize quite how badly this had affected me. I had been held down on the operating table while the anaesthetic was being administered, and I still look back on this as one of the worst experiences of my life. The feeling of losing consciousness was the same unreal sensation which dominated my anxiety attacks, and for years I would swear that at these times I could actually smell the anaesthetic gas. Hindsight tells me that no patient need have been treated in such a way even then; nowadays, of course, it would be out of the question.

I never went back to that dancing class, but a few weeks later the 'funny feeling' hit me in school assembly and I ran out of the hall to escape from the sensation. During the following weeks I thought of every excuse to miss morning prayers, but the unreal feelings then started to occur in other situations.

I dreaded the journey to school; I hated long walks or school outings and would think up any excuse to avoid them. It was only at home that I felt safe from the sensations which were so unpleasant and frightened me so much. But of course I had to go to school. I was 'nervy', they said, and I would have to learn to live with my feelings. Nowadays, psychiatrists would recognize separation anxiety in a highly-strung child with over-protective parents, also the trauma of the tonsils operation which had triggered off a phobic response in school situations; but this was the period just before the Second World War when most families were approaching a state of general upheaval and had little time to worry about nervy children.

Miraculously – or so it seemed to me – my symptoms disappeared after about six months. However, the following year, when I had forgotten all about them, they suddenly returned and from then on were part of my life while they lasted – usually for a period of a few weeks or months – before disappearing again, sometimes for two or three years.

Because of the war I was moved from one school to another, and the novelty of each new establishment seemed to help keep my anxiety feelings at bay. If I had remained at one school, it would have become obvious as the condition became established that I was not behaving normally, but I managed to hide the problem most of the time and just established a reputation for being difficult and withdrawn – and absent from school for minor reasons rather too often.

Even when I went to boarding school, where I felt I would have no travelling problems, the symptoms came back and affected me during services in chapel, on the games field and even in the classroom. When I could no longer hide my agitation, I started telling white lies when trying to explain what was wrong. I said I was suffering from delayed shell-shock after my (mostly imaginary) experiences during the 'Blitz'. This aroused a somewhat cynical reaction amongst the staff, who expressed their disapproval that my mother had not informed them of my unfortunate weakness. It did not make them particularly sympathetic, though it must have been apparent that I was disturbed and miserable.

I developed a habit of retreating into a fantasy world whenever I could; it was so much more comfortable and pleasant than the real one. However, the danger lay in sometimes making the mistake of letting the two worlds overlap. No young person could get away with this bizarre behaviour in these enlightened days: there would be medical examinations, interviews with psychologists and counselling sessions, but then I was regarded as a very peculiar girl and a *bad influence*!

The staff at my boarding school must have been very relieved when I persuaded my parents that I would be much happier at a day school instead of what I convinced them was the Dickensian establishment where they had placed me. They were horrified at the stories I told them about the dreadful things which went on in that very respectable and prestigious school – again products of my over-active imagination – and luckily for me, as my father was abroad and my mother had two younger children to cope with, there was little liaison between parents and teachers.

School phobia or agoraphobia? Looking back, I can see that in my case they were one and the same thing. I felt unsafe when the 'funny feelings' engulfed me and needed to escape from a situation, whether it was a maths lesson or a birthday party.

As a child who suffers from a physical disability has to learn to cope with it, so I managed to live with my phobia, hiding it as best I could and hoping each time there was a remission that the symptoms had gone for good.

During the periods of freedom I was still very anxiety-prone and had built up an extraordinary collection of other phobias. Perhaps 'phobia' in these cases is too strong a word – after all, a fear only becomes a phobia when it prevents the sufferer from living a normal life – but my fears certainly affected me very strongly and I would go out of my way to avoid everything which upset me. These included such things as balloons, skeletons, people with any deformity, hospitals, dentists' and doctors' surgeries, being blind-folded, hanging upside down (how I hated PE), travelling any distance, sleeping away from home, nose-bleeds, abstract thoughts, infinity, cemeteries, clouds, darkness, silence – the list was almost endless. There seemed to be so many upsetting things to cope with and I was only really happy in the fantasy world into which I slipped at every available opportunity.

Childhood fears

When I was eighteen, I felt that it was time to face up to my fears and learn to overcome them gradually. Life became much rosier, I did not need my daydreams so much and I began to feel like a normal person for the first time. The fears were fading and soon I had a job and a full social life.

Then, just after my twenty-first birthday, I had 'flu. Feeling a bit under par, I was waiting at a bus stop in the centre of London when the full range of half-forgotten sensations flooded over me. It had been so long since I had experienced the feelings of unreality and panic that I had forgotten how dreadful they were; I could not handle them and had to get a taxi home, where it took me the rest of the day to recover my equilibrium. I took a whole week off work, reasoning that I had not completely recovered from the 'flu and that the old symptoms had returned because of my poor state of health. However, the following Monday when I arrived at the same bus stop . . . back came the feelings of panic.

Every day from then on was a continual fight against rising panic and feelings of unreality. I had to reach the centre of London each day and every morning I felt sick with apprehension in anticipation of the journey. I was determined to hide my distress; I could not bear anyone to know about it and had a dread of making a fool of myself in front of other people, so I was determined not to draw attention to myself though I may have looked somewhat twitchy and uncomfortable to anyone who studied me carefully as I stood at the bus stop. I carried a piece of paper on which I had written my name, address, date and destination. When the real world started to slide and my memory played tricks, I would read this over and over again to reassure myself that I really existed.

I loved my job and dreaded the fact that I might have to give it up despite the misery of getting to the office each day. Sometimes when I felt really bad, I would think of looking for work nearer home, but I knew instinctively that once I gave in, the agoraphobia symptoms would follow me: then I would give up the local job and retreat into my home. I had to conquer the problem before it conquered me.

I combed libraries and bookshops looking for information about agoraphobia, but at that time there was very little written for the lay person and what I could find frightened me even more. I went to see a psychiatrist. 'You are probably really quite a nice young woman,' he told me! 'But you are obsessed with your symptoms which are caused by an anxiety state, and you will just have to learn to overcome them.' I had hoped that some sort of treatment might be available, but was warned off by the great man who felt that as I did not appear to have any underlying problems and was managing to cope – just – any treatment might result in aggravating the condition rather than curing it.

No treatment, just keep going! At least I had acquired one comforting piece of information: agoraphobia would not kill me and it would not ruin my life unless I let it. I am afraid there is no spectacular recovery to report – just four more years of working through it, learning to relax and not to be afraid of myself. It took me some time to realize that it was not the dreaded situations themselves which were the problem, but my own reactions to them.

Gradually it all faded; I hardly realized how much I was progressing until it became obvious that my nerves were no longer dominating my life. It takes some time to appreciate that one is really free. The biggest bonus was discovering that all the other anxieties also disappeared, until instead of being a permanently anxious person with many devastating fears, I discovered that I had become less fearful than most of the people I knew; that having trained myself not to worry, *I did not worry*. It is now twenty-seven years later and I have had no recurrence of any anxieties.

Two days after my article was published, I was sorting through piles of letters from sufferers, the main theme of all of them being, 'Thank God someone else knows how I feel!' Next day the BBC phoned to say that Woman's Hour was to broadcast a feature on agoraphobia and would I like to take part . . . Three hundred more letters arrived and I decided the only thing to do was to write a general letter and have it duplicated; including in it, apart from my own experiences, everything I knew about agoraphobia from what I had read and what I had learned from the few other agoraphobes I had met.

Three hundred letters were dispatched; three hundred came back, with more experiences, more views, more pleas for help and advice. 'The Open Door' came into being as a correspondence club and a regular monthly newsletter developed as TOD members pooled their knowledge and experience. Many of them wanted to contact fellow agoraphobes for mutual comfort and support, though the majority wished to remain anonymous, and soon we had area secretaries all over the country organizing local telephone contacts and even sufferers getting together in small groups when this was possible.

Soon 300 members became 3,000, pouring in to The Open Door as the result of articles in every national newspaper and woman's magazine; there were radio and television interviews and later even full-length documentaries. Doctors and psychiatrists became interested and I travelled all over the country speaking to groups in hospitals. Members of TOD were invited to take part in research projects, to try out different treatments and to fill in hundreds of questionnaires compiled by psychiatrists and psychologists who were writing books and papers on agoraphobia.

Eventually I withdrew from TOD after ten years for family reasons; I now had four children and a full-time job as a museum curator. During those ten years I had seen at least 60 per cent of TOD members make a good recovery and dispel the picture of the 'typical' agoraphobe spending the whole of her life in a housebound state in constant fear of the world outside.

Were those who recovered 'true' agoraphobes in the first

place, you may ask. Certainly some of the Open Door members whose condition was severe and appeared to resist all attempts to treat it, felt a sense of disbelief, almost a resentment when others wrote joyfully in the newsletters that their symptoms had faded and that life was great. Of course, many of these lucky ones were only mildly agoraphobic and some of them had never sought treatment of any kind, though their symptoms had at one time been distressing enough for them to seek help through The Open Door. It is very important to consider this group of mildly agoraphobic sufferers. The estimated number of 500,000 agoraphobes in the UK is based on those who are actually receiving treatment, but it is clear from TOD records and from the US and Canadian surveys referred to in the Introduction, that the total number must be considerably more than that.

Of course everyone is looking for the magic cure; the drug that will banish all unpleasant sensations, the revelation of a deep-seated psychological problem which will suddenly open the door to an anxiety-free life, the sudden spontaneous recovery. There are many ways in which each person can be helped and these will be examined in detail; but the way to recovery is moderately easy for some and seemingly almost insuperable for others. So much depends on each individual and her own unique problem.

If you run a splinter into your finger you may be able to remove it without much difficulty, but on the other hand it can disappear deep into the flesh causing pain and inflammation. The longer it remains the deeper it goes, the more painful it becomes and the more difficult it will eventually be for the doctor to remove it. The sooner agoraphobia is understood and the symptoms tackled, the greater the likelihood of a speedy recovery.

CHAPTER 3

Fear

*'Why I fear I know not; but yet as one deprived of sense
I fear all things.'*

Ovid

Our forebears had good reason to be fearful. In order to survive it was necessary for man to be continually on the alert for danger. Marauding tribes and dangerous animals on the prowl were a constant threat when you had only a club for a weapon and the sparse shelter of a cave to retreat into.

When danger threatens, the human body prepares for action as its anxiety response triggers off nervous chemical reactions. The heart beats faster, blood is shifted from other areas to limb muscles and to the brain, encouraging quick thinking and vigorous activity. Our cave man, his survival at risk, would be 'tensed up' and ready for action – to stand and fight or to run for his life.

Over the centuries as man has become more or less civilized, survival has become easier and most of the earlier dangers have disappeared. Of course modern man has his problems – mainly of his own making – but apart from those people for whom danger is a normal way of life, either in their profession or for entertainment, most of us are fairly assured of our survival to a ripe old age, bar accident or illness. The danger response is not now a necessary daily part of our bodily functions, so when it does occur it is likely to have longer-lasting disturbing effects. The cave man, victorious in battle or having escaped from a woolly mammoth or a sabre-tooth tiger for the umpteenth time, would relax and sleep by his fire, forgetting his nerveracking experience until the next time. Nowadays, the emotional consequences of a bad shock or accident will persist for much longer and, being unused to such experiences, we resent the effect they have on our well-being.

The Greeks believed that Phobos, the god of fear, could strike terror into the hearts of his victims and cause them to flee blindly into the clutches of Pan, the god with the ability to induce a state of uncontrolled behaviour in men and animals, a state of 'panic'. As we know, phobias and panic go hand in hand.

The Old English word *faer* meant 'sudden danger'. Fear is

Driven by Phobos into the clutches of Pan

what we experience when something unpleasant or dangerous is happening to us; without any conscious effort, our body immediately reacts by producing the sensations which often we interpret as equally unpleasant as the cause. However, there are people who actually enjoy these sensations, finding them exciting and stimulating and frequently seeking a career or hobby where there is an element of danger. A certain amount of fear is healthy and prevents us from risking ourselves in dangerous situations, but there are many of us who – because of our personalities – are more prone to fears than others.

Anxiety is the permanent companion of so many of us. The Latin word *anxius* meant 'to press tightly or to strangle'; the dictionary defines it as a state of chronic apprehension. Men and women and are blessed – some may say cursed – with imagination; they can project their thoughts into the future and anticipate what *might* happen rather than what actually *will* happen . . . and what misery this can cause!

Anxiety comes in several different forms. If we know what is worrying us – the safety of a child, for instance – this is called *attached anxiety*. Thinking about a visit to the dentist is anticipatory or *signal anxiety*. When the problem is chronic apprehension and nervousness without any specific reason, this is *free-floating anxiety*; and finally, the anxiety about something which we know is not threatening but which terrifies us all the same, is *phobic anxiety*.

A phobia is a fear which is severe enough to alter or seriously disturb the sufferer's life. The object of the fear, or the situation in which the person experiences irrational fear, has to be avoided at all costs. Many specific phobias are of animals; snakes are the most feared creatures of all, closely followed by spiders, cats and birds, but virtually anything can become the object of someone's phobia. You may remember how some years ago a businessman on a television programme admitted to a phobia of large leaves; his route to work was carefully planned so that he did not have to drive along leafy lanes in the summer and he considered his next-door neighbour anti-social because he grew rhubarb in his garden. Another instance was a policeman who admitted to a phobia of navels and could never sit on a beach or go to a public swimming pool.

Ornithophobia

Members of The Open Door, though mostly sufferers from agoraphobia, also produced some surprising phobias. One woman went out to visit friends late one evening; somehow the conversation turned to space travel, the earth spinning on its axis and the effects of gravity. On her way home Mrs P. was overcome by the thought of the size of the universe and, looking up at the star-filled sky, felt as though she was spinning off the face of the Earth. After that alarming experience, she did not leave her house for nine years.

Two TOD members had foot phobias and another had a phobia about babies' hands. A woman with a 'purple' phobia could not bear to catch sight of anything that colour. One rather sad thing I discovered was that so many people were intolerant of others' phobias. 'Frightened of babies' hands, what a silly woman!' said one TOD member whose own dread of thunderstorms caused her to plan her life around each day's weather forecast.

Weather affects many people. You have only to watch a cat's behaviour during a storm to appreciate how a sensitive nervous system can react to changes in atmospheric pressure. The fear of thunderstorms is one of the most common 'nature' phobias, but clouds, wind, snow or mist can have a devastating effect on other phobic people. Even a clear sunny day can be distressing to someone who finds the sight of a vast open sky quite unnerving.

Social phobias are often difficult to separate from agoraphobia. Agoraphobes avoid eating in restaurants because of the sensation of being trapped; those with social phobias cannot bear being looked at and find it difficult to eat or drink in front of others – even, in extreme cases, their own family. The fear of blushing is another social phobia which can cause the sufferer to avoid meeting or talking to other people. Many actions cause distress for those with a social phobia; reading out loud, writing in front of another person or even using the telephone are all problems that can seem unsurmountable.

Another common fear is of vomiting; someone with such a phobia will avoid travelling if this produces feelings of nausea and will eat only food which can be trusted not to upset the stomach. This makes life unadventurous but bearable. Surprisingly, the person who has a phobia of *someone else* vomiting has a greater problem, since there is no way they can control the situation. Children and pets are prone to throw up without warning, causing acute anguish to the sick-phobic sufferer who can even be thrown into a state of panic if someone burps, chokes or has a coughing fit which might possibly lead to vomiting.

An anxiety state may produce unpleasant physical symptoms which can convince the patient that she is suffering from some specific disease. Unlike a true hypochondriac who may actually enjoy thinking she is ill, the person with an illness phobia is in constant dread of contracting a particular disease, imagining she has all the symptoms even when repeatedly assured that she is perfectly healthy.

How many people say at one time or another, 'I have a terrible phobia about dentists.' They haven't, of course – they are just experiencing a natural apprehension which is soon forgotten after the 'ordeal' of the treatment. So many folk are unnerved by the thought of hospitals, doctors and dentists that sometimes they begin to have an inkling of what true phobia sufferers endure. It is amazing what a phobic person will put up with rather than face up to the dread of consulting a doctor or dentist; they will even pull out their own teeth rather than experience the dentist's chair. One TOD member insisted that any reference to dentists be cut out of her newsletters, because even the printed word *dentist* caused her to panic.

Blood phobias are very common; though many of us are squeamish about the sight of blood, someone with a severe blood phobia may actually faint, even if the blood flowing is tomato ketchup in a television play! Fear of injections may also induce a fainting attack; a snap survey amongst TOD members discovered that men outnumbered women by three to one when it came to hypodermic horrors.

There are people who actively enjoy the physical sensations of fear and deliberately expose themselves to dangerous situations – sometimes making a career out of it and frequently indulging in hair-raising activities in the name of sport or adventure. Most of us are ashamed to admit we might be nervous or fearful, since courage has always been considered to be a superior virtue and from childhood we are told to be brave and not show fear. There can be a backlash though, because some people – particularly boys – are so conditioned to be 'brave' that they become over-confident, foolhardy and accident-prone.

Many of the world's great heroes might have lived to fight another day if they had been less fearless and more cautious. At the Battle of Trafalgar, Nelson insisted on wearing all his medals and decorations so that the enemy could identify and marvel at the bold British admiral . . . they made a great target for a French sniper, and the man who in his youth had remarked, 'Fear? What is it?' returned to his homeland pickled in a keg of brandy instead of sailing back in triumph.

Better a live coward than a dead hero

CHAPTER 4

Who are the Sufferers?

'His sisters and his cousins and his aunts'
                    W. S. Gilbert, *HMS Pinafore*

Phobias are not a phenomenon of modern life; through the ages people have suffered from a variety of phobias, but it is interesting to find that there are few historical references to a woman being affected. Dr Mitchell notes, 'This does not mean that women did not suffer from them but probably reflects the sexist bias that only events happening to man are worthy to be recorded!' A notable exception was Maria de Medici, who died in 1842. Although she loved flowers, she could not bear roses and felt faint if she saw one even in a painting.

Apparently there was no shame attached to a man admitting to a specific phobia, but when agoraphobia became recognized with its background and sudden panics, it quickly came to be considered a woman's problem. Described until recently as the 'housebound housewife's complaint' or the 'empty nest syndrome', it was linked with menopausal women whose children had left home and whose husbands had better things to do than encourage such neurotic behaviour as the women sat at home anxious and bored, with little to do but brood over imaginary symptoms. This is a very out-of-date concept, but the

stigma still persists and it is little wonder that many agoraphobic men dislike being identified with the condition.

The womb and the mysteries surrounding it: childbirth,
the menstrual cycle, the menopause and general gynaeco-
logical problems – have all been blamed throughout the
ages for the state of a woman's mental health. Plato believed
that the womb or *hysteros* ardently desired to produce
children; if it remained sterile for long after puberty, it
became indignant, dissatisfied and ill-tempered; then it
started to wander round the body, causing mischief or
hysteria. Four hundred years ago Hippocrates said, 'I advise
maidens who suffer from hysteria to marry as soon as
possible; for if they conceive they will be cured.'

Man, not having a womb, could not possibly be troubled
by the irrational anxieties or hysterical panics from which
some women suffered; if he happened to find himself similarly afflicted, he naturally did his best to conceal such
unmanly symptoms.

It is estimated that 20 per cent of agoraphobes are men,
but again this figure is based on the number of men seeking
treatment and does not take into account the secret sufferers
who are battling on, determined to lead a normal life. Many
have a horror of anyone knowing about their phobia, as
there is often a definite possibility of jobs being at risk and
careers being ruined if the 'weakness' is exposed. There
were a number of well-known people in The Open Door –
television and other media personalities, an eminent lawyer,
several doctors and even a Member of Parliament. All
wished to remain anonymous and had no contact with other
TOD members – a pity, as some of them could have
contributed much to the newsletters and by publicizing the
fact that agoraphobia sufferers are normal people and not
neurotic invalids.

There are, of course, a few recorded incidences of male
agoraphobes – including, of all people, Sigmund Freud who

for several years had a fear of travelling and became so anxious that he would arrive at a station an hour before the train was due to leave. A professor of English at Cambridge suffered from agoraphobia for forty-eight years, managing to hide this from colleagues and students and never seeking medical help. Only his family and close friends knew of his condition, though it may well have been noted by others that the only way he could cross the college quadrangle was by sidling round the sides with his back to the wall.

An American professor wrote in 1928:

> Let me assume that I am walking down University Drive by the Lake. I am a normal man for the first quarter of a mile; for the next hundred yards I am in a mild state of dread, controllable and controlled; for the next twenty yards in an acute state of dread, yet controlled; for the next ten, in an anguish of terror that hasn't reached the crisis of explosion; and in a half-dozen steps more I am in as fierce a panic of isolation from help and home and of immediate death as a man overboard in mid-Atlantic or on a window ledge far up in a sky-scraper with flames lapping his shoulders.
>
> It is as scientific a fact as any I know that my phobic seizures at their worst approach any limits of terror that the human mind is capable of in the actual presence of death in its most horrible forms.

In a survey of 2,300 women in TOD, it was found that the average age of an agoraphobe was thirty-two years. The youngest person taking part in the survey was thirteen, the oldest eighty-seven. The most common reason for the onset of the phobia was 'age' according to the doctors; note that any idea of sex equality goes out of the window where GPs are concerned!

Teenagers	Adolescence; you'll grow out of it.
Early twenties	You will find it will improve when you get married.

25–36 (single)	As above, coupled with the remark, 'It's about time you found yourself a husband.'
25–35 (married)	Effort of running a home and caring for the family. You'll feel better when they go to school/grow up/leave home.
35–65	The menopause – a favourite reason. Dozens of young women in their thirties are told they are going through an 'early change'.
65 onwards	Old age. Slow down, keep taking the tablets, don't bother to make an effort.

A similar survey amongst 220 men showed that the average age of the male agoraphobe was fifty – but none of them was told that the phobias were due to their age!

Agoraphobia usually develops between the ages of 18 and 35 years, according to the major surveys which have been carried out. It is rare for it to start in childhood according to the psychiatrists, but in fact we shall see that many children do suffer from agoraphobia although it may not be recognized as such.

Men have a particularly hard struggle to hide the fact that they are agoraphobic. Because it is imperative that they hold down a job and support their families, they are less likely to become housebound to the same extent as married women at home. There is no opportunity to retreat into the home, so the agoraphobic habit is not built up to the same degree. However difficult life may be, it is neither financially possible nor socially acceptable – even in these liberated days when house-husbands run a few middle-class homes – for a man to suffer from a nervous illness; so when he does seek treatment, he will do so at a much earlier stage than a woman would and, because he is more highly motivated to recover, the success rate is higher than in the case of a woman. I have made the comparison with *married* women here, as their single sisters have many of the same problems as men with regard to careers and finances; they do not have the excuse to stay at home because of family commitments, so are forced to keep going. Again, the proportion of single women who recover is higher than that of married women; they are more likely to persevere with treatment because career and lifestyle are in jeopardy, therefore they will make more effort to overcome the problem however distressing it may be.

Not surprisingly, the highest number of single women agoraphobes occurs in the age group 50–70, where a person may be forced to give up her job in order to care for elderly parents. As much restricted and tied to the home as the mother of young children, her agoraphobic condition – which may have been controlled or lain dormant for many years – flares up and takes over her life.

Ross Mitchell in *Phobias* says:

> Although there is no specific pre-phobic personality type, people will be more likely to develop a phobia the more they are anxiety-prone, sensitive to external and internal pressures and generally lacking in self-confidence. For some people the ground is prepared from birth onwards; they grow up to be more sensitive, anxious and insecure. They carry the potential to be afraid and experience panic and want to avoid circumstances which they have come to realise evoke such feelings.

Obviously those people who are anxiety-prone and lacking in self-confidence will naturally opt for a lifestyle which presents the least threat.

Married women in the 20–35 age range constitute the largest group of acute agoraphobia sufferers and it is easy to see why. Despite feminist propaganda, for many girls of a nervous disposition the idea of marriage and the pleasant restrictions of motherhood is vastly preferable to the stresses of a career and the need to compete in the world outside home. Unfortunately, pregnancy and confinement may aggravate an anxiety state and, finding herself tied to the house with a baby, the young mother can find genuine excuses to avoid going out more than is absolutely necessary – a sure way to develop agoraphobic habits.

Unfortunately for the agoraphobic mother, children grow up and want to be independent. If she has allowed herself to become housebound, she may in extreme cases try to keep the children at home with her when they should be in school. Her husband will have to take care of all the chores outside the home such as shopping, ensuring the children get to school and taking them to keep medical and dental appointments. This is a particularly gloomy picture and the average mother usually manages to keep going, though she does rely heavily on the support of her family; if they understand her condition, their help will be vital in encouraging her steps towards recovery.

I have seven children so it has been very difficult to keep much from any of them. My agoraphobia came just after the last child was born six years ago, but each of my children has accepted my trouble without question. As they get older I am able to explain more fully the trouble I have with getting out. When school speech days arrive I explain to the children that I will get there if I possibly can and because they understand the effort I have to make they never blame me if I can't make it at the last minute. I feel guilty enough as it is and am grateful for their understanding and acceptance.

Frances.

Unfortunately many stay-at-home mothers fail to appreciate the problems that may lie ahead when the family leave the nest and they are stuck in the maternal rut.

. . . These built-in fears and horrors are very little removed from the instinctive avoidance reaction in animals that serve to steer them away from unfavourable situations and maintain them in their correct environment . . . Most women fortunately have an instinct to stay at home, especially when their maternal instinct is active, and what chaos there would be if this were not so. It is a genuine instinctive attachment to 'base' that keeps us happily pottering around garden and house, not primarily a fear of the outside world.

Nancy.

The day dawns for many agoraphobes when the outside world has to be faced and the longer this day is postponed, the harder it will be to make the effort. One 21-year-old boy decided he would not be beaten:

I was desperate to find any job and applied for a post on the London Underground, though I thought I would probably not stick to it for more than a few days. My family in Bristol was against the idea as they knew the state of my nerves, but being rather impulsive and obstinate I was all the more determined to see it through . . . In nineteen months I have been badly panicky only three times, but in each case I was able to fake a sick headache and make a quick exit to the fresh air outside where it doesn't take but a few minutes to get back to normal. Every day I get a little more confident.

This approach is known as counterphobic behaviour. Professor Isaac Marks states, 'This is the attraction some patients have to their phobic situation or object so that they seek it out repeatedly . . . Counterphobic behaviour may thus help the patient overcome his fear by gradually familiarising him with the phobia until it loses its frightening aspect . . .'

'Habits are at first cobwebs, at last cables.' (Proverb)

Aunt Aggie has not left the house for forty years. It is Aunt Aggie's fate that every agoraphobe dreads and as we saw earlier, the way in which the general public and the media perceive the condition.

One of our most eminent psychiatrists had an aunt who became agoraphobic after an accident with a tram fifty years ago. She refused to go out when she recovered from her injuries, thus building up a habit of staying at home until it became impossible to break.

I have already mentioned Dickens' novel *Great Expectations* where Miss Havisham, an elderly recluse, has been housebound since being jilted at the altar many years before. Dressed in her wedding finery and living in a dilapidated house with cobwebs covering the mouldering remains of her wedding feast, Miss Havisham typifies the picture of the eccentric agoraphobe. What is typical is that Miss Havisham became housebound as the result of a nasty shock; she had no more interest in the outside world, and her home – however grim and dreary – was her sanctuary. Mind you, she developed into a pretty unpleasant character determined to disrupt other people's lives, a sorry trait of some long-term sufferers who lose close contact with their fellow men and women.

Children suffer too

Refusal to go to school is sometimes called school phobia, but many experts feel that it is not a true phobia. Dr Mitchell says:

> The separation anxiety and the uncertainty about fitting in with strange teachers and with schoolfellows are understandable if

undesirable. Further, the children are normally not avoiding school as such, but are trying to avoid separation from home and parents.

Isaac Marks feels that this is too one-sided a view: 'Many children are more afraid of the school than of leaving their mothers. Some are afraid both of school and of separation from their parents.'

What are they frightened of at school?

In Professor Marks' opinion:

> Young children may give no reason at all for their refusal. Older children will attribute their fears to various aspects of school life. They may complain of being bullied or teased or of being self-conscious about their appearance . . . anxiety about doing badly at games or school work or fear of a teacher may be mentioned. A few children are frightened that harm may befall their mother while they are at school.

In many cases, developing agoraphobia is the real problem. The reasons these children offer for their fears at school are often just excuses because they cannot describe what it is that really upsets them.

When I was a child going through one of my 'bad' patches, I would be asked by exasperated teachers and worried parents, '*Why* don't you want to go to school; what are you afraid of?'. They could not understand why I found it impossible to explain, because I knew it was my feelings and my reactions to certain situations which were upsetting me and it is very difficult for a child to understand itself, never mind trying to explain to adults. No, I was not frightened of anything in particular, but a pack of noisy children on the move could seem overwhelming to one who

School phobia

preferred to stay quietly in one place. There was this need to escape – from the other children; the frightening surge of the crowd when a bell sounded; the overpowering sense of being trapped in the assembly hall; the feeling of tension which could build up in a lesson when you were stuck at a desk in the class-room, unable to break the tension by slipping out of the room for a few moments.

A 'physical' child will get rid of its energy in the playground, on the sports field, in the gymnasium, but the quieter one may be left with a lot of bottled-up tension and no way of working it off. Disliking to be naughty or noisy in class, the tension can become unbearable and trying to concentrate on the lesson may be impossible. The instinct is then to break away from the pack of children, the discipline of the class-room, the ordeal of assembly. Because it is not possible to escape, the obvious thing is to avoid these situations in future. Worrying about these fears, a child will develop physical symptoms such as nausea, sore throat, abdominal pains – real symptoms which cause increased distress, and if not handled correctly can mean even more problems in the future.

If school phobia persists and is not treated, it may develop into more recognizable agoraphobia, and an adolescent agoraphobe is in a sorry plight, particularly if she becomes housebound. Lack of contact with other teenagers may result in the phobic girl retreating into daydreams and fantasies: living her life through books and television and avoiding contact with the real world outside her home. It is particularly difficult to persuade adolescents to take part in any treatment programme, as recovery means having to face up to the problems of normal everyday life.

CHAPTER 5

Is there a Cure?

*'Recovery lies not so much in the absence of symptoms as
in knowing how to cope with those present.'*
Dr Claire Weekes

Some people will tell you that complete recovery from
agoraphobia is not possible; that the best you can hope for is
partial control of the worst symptoms, but with the probability of recurrence always hanging over you so that you
can never be completely free of the problem. This depressing
point of view is usually put forward by long-term agoraphobes who have adjusted to a restricted life pattern which
suits them and makes few demands upon them, physically
or emotionally.

There are many sufferers who are prepared to sit tight at
home, waiting for their doctor to prescribe the magic pill
which will immediately banish all fears and unpleasant
symptoms. Unfortunately this will never happen and you
must face up to it. You cannot *cure* a habit with drugs and
agoraphobia is a habit. *You* have to work at your recovery,
just as a fat person must stick to his diet or an alcoholic
tackle his drinking problem. No matter what treatment is
available to you, nothing will work without your coopera-
tion and determination to lead a normal life. Of course you
need help, and although there are still too few family
doctors who really understand the condition and have the

time to become involved with therapy, more and more hospitals are providing specialist treatment and support in psychiatric units and day centres.

Though it is true that drugs do not constitute a magic cure for agoraphobia, there are times – particularly when there is a background of acute anxiety or depression – when drugs can provide emergency help.

During the 1960s, it became fashionable to keep a bottle of tranquillizers in the medicine cupboard and turn to them in times of stress. Coping with children, marriage problems, an argument with a neighbour – all became a reason for a woman to swallow a pill with a cup of tea, knowing that although it would not remove the cause of her stress it would at least calm her nerves and help her to face the situation.

Everyone, patients and doctors alike, began to regard tranquillizers as the answer to any problem caused by anxiety, stress and emotional upheavals. These drugs were a real boon for the overworked doctors who could rarely spare the time needed to counsel patients, but who were thankful to prescribe indefinitely for those who wanted to continue to take pills. The trouble was that instead of being used to help themselves over a crisis, nervous people began to regard their pills as a permanent crutch to assist them to limp through life. It was hardly surprising that problems began to arise and patients who had been taking their 'happy' pills over a long period found themselves dependent upon them; once the beneficial effects wore off, they were faced with having to cope with withdrawal symptoms as well as the original situation.

There is no doubt that there are drugs which will relieve symptoms, alleviate anxiety and often have a quite miraculous effect upon the patient, who feels she can begin to lead a normal life. However, problems will arise when the drug is discontinued, unless the agoraphobe has learned how to cope with the setbacks which will inevitably arise if her attitude is still to avoid panic rather than to conquer it. We all have to face the fact that life *is* stressful and if we are under the influence of tranquillizing drugs and in a false state of serenity, our bodies have no drive to tackle the situation. We can continue to avoid a problem, but avoiding it does not make it go away. In most cases we should regard anxiety as a spur to action, an unpleasant experience whose function it is to get us moving.

Tranquillizers are most effective if they are taken only when you really need them. One GP says:

> They are not only useful for coping with a bad patch but they are of real help to those who are chronically anxious. I have a programme of putting such patients on an intermittent dosage and tell patients the maximum amount they can take in a week – but that they should take them only when they know they are going to have a particularly anxious time and even then to take as few as possible. Their dosage goes up and down accordingly; they don't just take the pills automatically, they stop and consider whether they have reached the peak of desperation where they cannot do without them. It is a good long-term therapy.

I must mention here that when I was just starting to recover from my longest, most harrowing (and final) period of agoraphobia in my twenties, tranquillizers made their first appearance on the market. One of the earliest was called *Oblivon* and for a short time it was possible to buy these at a chemist's without a prescription. Marvellous, I thought; here is my lifeline. I bought a bottle and kept it in my handbag. I never took one single pill, but the mere fact of knowing they were there made me feel better. I imagine I felt that if I did take one during a bad panic attack and it did not work, I would be so demoralized that I would give up. Instead, being convinced that I had a 'miracle cure' which would work if things got really bad, I never felt desperate enough to try it out.

General practitioners

In an ideal situation, the understanding GP will explain the condition, removing fears of insanity and ominous physical diseases and giving sensible advice and treatment. In so many cases, unfortunately, the doctor himself does not understand agoraphobia and can add to the patient's distress by adopting the all-too-familiar 'Snap-out-of-it' attitude. Too often the problem has to do with lack of communication when the doctor has little time to deal with a patient who seems incapable of explaining her problem coherently.

> My GP is a kind but bluff fatherly type who has little time for 'nervy' women. He talks *at* me but won't give me a chance to explain, so I come away from the surgery feeling I have got nowhere. I try to tell him about my nerves and he launches into a three-minute lecture supposed to be reassuring but which just makes me feel guilty about making a fuss.
>
> Miriam (27) single.

'I cannot discuss anything with my doctor,' is a typical protest. 'There is never the time to explain, and if I *have* managed to make the journey to his surgery and had to sit in the waiting room, I am in such a state that I can't remember half the things I wanted to say.'

In these days very few doctors will make a house call except in a case of emergency, and it is terribly difficult for an agoraphobic person not only to face the ordeal of a visit to the surgery, but to be able to discuss the condition coherently when they get there. In years gone by, patients looked upon their family doctor as a friend and counsellor, but doctors now have little time to live up to that image. Worse still, a good many are downright unsympathetic to those whom they consider to be neurotic and have little inclination to go into the problem in any depth.

'Getting through' to your doctor

One way to tackle the difficulty of lack of communication is to put everything down on paper and send your case history to the doctor before making an appointment to see him. Stick to the facts and try not to indulge in self-pity as you list your symptoms, explaining how your life is being affected by agoraphobia. Wait a day or two before making your appointment, thus giving the doctor time to digest your letter and consider your problem before seeing you personally. With the information available, your doctor should be able to put you at ease and you will be more relaxed at not having to face a barrage of questions . . .

You are (outwardly) composed as you sit in the surgery; the doctor has your notes in front of him so that he has a basis to work from and is now in a position to make some constructive suggestions about treatment.

First of all, it is important to establish that there is nothing physically wrong with you; that the wretched symptoms which are so upsetting are the product of your over-sensitized nervous system and not a warning of some dreaded disease. The majority of sufferers are convinced that they have weak hearts or some frightening mental illness, until they begin to understand the nature of agoraphobia.

Suppose you have been lucky enough to discover your doctor is sympathetic and does understand; has information about and access to treatment for you; has prescribed, if he thinks it is in your best interest for the moment, tranquillizers to damp down the worst of the anxiety and has promised to refer you for specialist treatment. What is your next step?

Yes, help is available in your area, you are told. Now it is crunch time. It is all well and good sitting at home feeling that nothing is being done for agoraphobia sufferers: no one understands and nothing will help. Now you are faced with doing something about it – *you*, not the doctor. You are told that treatment is available and you have to make an effort to achieve recovery – if that is what you really want . . .

TOD members would write to tell me why they had not been able to attend therapy sessions, concluding that of course they could never recover as everything was against them. It was not their fault, naturally, but they had responsibilities to their children; the journey to the treatment centre was impossible; their husbands were unsympathetic and would not help . . . and so on.

If treatment is available and you really want to get better, you will find some way – like Mrs Mac. from Edinburgh, a TOD member who had read about treatment at St Bartholomew's Hospital in London.

I had not been out of the house on my own for nearly a year – when I did go out with my husband, it had to be after dark. When I read in the newsletter about Dr F's offer to help TOD members, something just snapped. I packed a case and phoned for a cab and just took off to catch the overnight train.

I couldn't believe it was really me buying a ticket and getting on a train. Everything was so unreal anyway that the usual feelings of unreality didn't matter any more – I felt quite high and giggly!

A taxi got me to the hospital early in the morning and I just waited until Dr F arrived for his clinic. Everyone was surprised, and I think impressed at the effort I had made and it was agreed I should spend three days at the hospital while a desensitization programme was drawn up for me to carry out at home. In the meantime I started treatment at the hospital.

No, I am not cured by some miracle but my self-confidence has doubled and I am working on the programme and already showing considerable progress. It is really amazing what you can do if you really try.

So . . . you are determined to get better, but you find that your GP can offer little help and you are back to square one. Do you give in? Of course not: you telephone or write to the psychiatric department at your nearest hospital and ask if they have a therapy programme for agoraphobic patients. You can then inform your doctor that help is available and ask him for a letter of referral, even if he tries to tell you that you do not need specialist treatment, that you are a perfectly normal person and not a psychiatric case . . . yes, there are doctors who say this.

If your local hospital cannot help, contact your Health Centre, the Samaritans, Citizens Advice Bureau or any of the other helping agencies and ask them if they will assist you to find out where treatment may be available.

Still no help? Write to the advice pages of any woman's magazine or national newspaper and explain your dilemma.

They will have addresses of self-help groups and phobia organizations currently in existence – there may even be one in your own area. These bodies will certainly be able to advise you.

Treatment

What can you expect when you present yourself for treatment? *Not* ECT for a start. One of the reasons why so many agoraphobes refused to seek treatment in the past was that they knew that the condition was frequently treated by electro-convulsive therapy. Twenty years ago when it was assumed that agoraphobia was automatically linked with depression, many people underwent shock treatment for something they did not suffer from – it did nothing for their phobia. Depressed? Of course they were depressed; they were faced with the possibility of becoming permanently housebound and no one could explain to them exactly what was the matter. In the majority of cases the depression was caused by the agoraphobia, not vice-versa.

Dr Ross Mitchell in *Phobias* states:

> ECT has no place in the treatment of primary phobias but may be indicated in severe depressive illnesses in which there can occasionally be phobic symptoms. Here the electrical treatment is directed to the depressive illnesses and not to the phobic symptoms themselves.

Of course there are agoraphobes who suffer from depression. There are people with serious psychiatric disorders and personality problems who are agoraphobic. There are also others with hay fever, tennis elbow, haemorrhoids or bunions who suffer from agoraphobia. They all need treatment for their various disorders, but in this book we are concentrating solely on the *habit* of agoraphobia, not what *may* have caused it or what may accompany it.

There is a school of thought which feels that the cause of agoraphobia must be identified before the patient can be helped through analysis and psychotherapy, and it is obvious that if someone is seriously disturbed, psychotherapy will be a vital part of their treatment. However, based on the questionnaire completed by every TOD member, it appears that most agoraphobics can pinpoint the onset of their condition to a time following a major upset in their lives.

In *Living with Fear*, Isaac Marks says:

> There is no need to look for hidden origins to phobias and obsessions. They do not point to dark, unconscious secrets which have to be uncovered for treatment to succeed. The anxieties can be cleared by working on the assumption that the sufferer needs to get used to the situation which troubles him, without any need to reconstruct his personality.

Ten per cent of the original TOD members – the wealthy ones – had been undergoing psychoanalysis in the hope that their phobia would disappear once the cause had been discovered. Ten, twenty years had gone by in some cases and recovery seemed no nearer, though they had learned some interesting facts about themselves. As one member explained: 'My analyst says I'm afraid to go out in case I see a bus. A bus is a phallic symbol, you see, and Dr X says my problem is basically a sexual one.' This woman had spent a month in hospital some fifteen years earlier after being knocked down by a bus; her agoraphobia had developed soon afterwards.

Those of us who have emerged from the shadows of agoraphobia know that there is only one way to tackle it, and that is by exposure to the situations which you feel you cannot face – exposure to the situations *and* exposure to the

Freudian symbol

unpleasant symptoms. Agoraphobes are inclined to judge their progress on their ability not to feel panic. Two or three panic-free trips to the supermarket and they feel they are doing really well; then on the next occasion the old dreaded feelings come flooding back and it is back to square one again.

Behaviour Therapy

In one form or another this is now accepted as the most successful way of treating agoraphobia. It is based on the theory that phobias have become a habit which can be corrected by unlearning the old habit and relearning new ones to replace it. The agoraphobic person has learnt to react wrongly in certain situations, so must be retrained to react correctly and without fear.

The technique which the behavioural therapists still consider to be the most effective and quickest way to overcome phobias is known as *flooding*, which is a pretty good description since it is comparable with being pushed into the deep end of a swimming pool when you cannot swim. You (probably) learn to swim quite quickly, but it is not a pleasant experience!

The theory is that the patient is exposed to her most dreaded situation and encouraged to remain within it, experiencing the most unpleasant sensations that her phobia can produce, facing the panic and distress until the peak is past and the terrifying symptoms gradually evaporate. This might take a few minutes, or it might take an hour or two, but the important point is that the sufferer stands her ground until the anxiety starts to lessen, and has to be prepared to remain until it does.

The agoraphobe's greatest dread is that her system cannot tolerate the acute phase of a panic attack; that there must be some terrible climax which will prove fatal. This is not so; when the panic feelings reach a peak there is only one way they can go – down. They will gradually subside and the sufferer will find herself sick and shaky but still in one piece . . . and a step nearer recovery.

There is no doubt that such an experience is more exhausting than exhilarating, but it cannot be denied that *if the patient is well prepared by her therapist and has the motivation and the courage to cooperate, this can be one of the fastest ways to overcome agoraphobia.*

Even if this type of therapy were readily available throughout the country, the majority of those needing treatment could not take advantage of it. Tense and hypersensitive, in a state of chronic anxiety, for them the prospect of the flooding ordeal would be out of the question. The very thought of participating in treatment of any kind can be distressing to someone whose over-active imagination causes her to anticipate and experience the unpleasant symptoms that strike in her phobic situations.

'I try so hard to fight it,' sufferers say, as though they were about to go into battle. *Fight?* You can just imagine them clenching their fists, gritting their teeth, breathing fast and building up so much nervous energy in their determination to overcome any feelings of panic that the tension becomes unbearable and their brave resolutions are defeated. Anticipating fear in the mind is equivalent to experiencing fear in reality, and the average agoraphobe – with the over-active imagination which is frequently part of the phobic personality – is permanently exposed to dreaded situations, living in them day and night. Is this not a type of flooding? If flooding is meant to help, why has she not been able to cure herself long ago?

'Once we confront our fear determinedly it will diminish', writes Professor Marks. 'If we do not understand the fear we cannot confront it, we continually run away from it and not having the knowledge to tackle it positively we are overwhelmed.'

Systematic Desensitization
This form of behaviour therapy has proved the most acceptable technique to date. The first part of the treatment concentrates on helping the patient to achieve a state of complete relaxation, and this is no easy feat where agoraphobic people are concerned. For a start, the effort of making the journey to the hospital or day centre often results in the patient arriving in a state of nervous exhaustion, with the prospect of the return trip home after treatment another ordeal to be faced.

Tense and nervous people have forgotten how to relax and have to be taught this skill through exercise and deep breathing techniques. The phobic person finds this very difficult; the idea of 'letting go' is frightening when your whole life is concentrated on trying to control your emotions. To lie on a couch and submit to another person's instructions may actually increase the tension. It is the old story of feeling trapped; instinct tells you to open your eyes, sit up, put your feet on the floor and get out quick!

Perseverance and a sympathetic therapist will gradually overcome the patient's aversion and then the next stage can be tackled. As we have seen, a vivid imagination can cause an immense amount of distress and it is important to channel the imagination in the right direction. From constantly visualizing phobic situations and experiencing the accompanying physical symptoms and mental distress, the patient is encouraged to imagine places and situations in which she would feel comfortable, the therapist encouraging her to experience feelings of peace and tranquillity. Sometimes music or tapes of familiar loved sounds or voices may be played in the background. If one can learn the techniques of relaxation, create an imaginary haven to drift into instead of the nightmare of out-of-control negative thoughts and fantasies, the first step to recovery has been taken.

When the outside world is a threatening place it can be attractive, once she has acquired the knack, for an agoraphobe to retreat more and more into a fantasy life where anxieties disappear. This is particularly evident with children and adolescents and can lead to permanent withdrawal if not controlled. The next step for the therapist is to make the imagination work towards a positive goal, and persuade the patient to imagine a mildly unpleasant situation, at the same time consciously holding on to the feelings of calm that her happier mind-pictures produce. Once she can face this situation with the minimum of distress, she will be encouraged to tackle a more difficult one, gradually progressing through her dreaded places until she can visualize herself coping with the situation she feels it would be impossible to face in real life.

Desensitization in fantasy is a long-drawn-out procedure and when possible, treatment is speeded up by persuading the patient to tackle the initial step – the mildly upsetting situation – first in imagination and then in reality. Between treatment sessions she must practise facing the problems every day, remaining relaxed and calm as she has been taught. When she is ready she will take the next step, and from there will gradually progress through her list of black spots until she reaches her goal – the place she dreads the most.

Back in the early years of The Open Door, members wrote enthusiastically in the newsletter about their experiences with desensitization therapy. For many of them this seemed to be the answer, though it was frustrating for those who had no treatment facilities in their particular area. Success stories were circulated as patients gingerly emerged through their front doors, walked to the next house, to the corner of the street, to the shops. It looked as though many of them were on the way to recovery:

> 'I haven't had a panic for weeks . . .'
> 'I can face the supermarket without dreading a return
>   of the old feelings.'
> 'Sat right through the church service feeling great.'

But the euphoria did not last and sooner or later the majority of the desensitization patients started backsliding. What was wrong? They had thought that by learning to relax and remaining calm they could avoid panics and that their previous unpleasant symptoms had gone for good. Unfortunately, sooner or later they found that this was not the case; moving around freely, anxiety gradually faded to mild apprehension and confidence was returning when out of the blue the old panic struck once more and the patient found herself distressed, disappointed and determined not to venture out again. All the efforts to get back to normal had ended in failure. Agoraphobia was still there.

Sadly, many of these people refused to try again; they could not accept the fact that it is a necessary part of recovery to experience the panics and all the accompanying symptoms, in order to learn how to cope with them and eventually overcome them. Nowadays, patients are left in little doubt before they start treatment that they must learn to face their fears, and the outcome of their efforts is considerably more successful.

Another behaviour therapy technique involved patients being taken out individually or in groups, by therapists who were able to give the necessary support and encouragement to those trying to cope with anxiety and panic and lead them through a series of difficult situations. They went to busy town centres, travelled on buses and trains, queued in shops and pushed through crowds. These exercises proved helpful in that the patients were given the chance of experiencing phobic problems with professional support. But the agoraphobe is an odd bird. Some feel bad in any and every situation, but others have very definite trouble spots peculiar to themselves. It is difficult to explain why one side of a road feels hostile and the other 'safe'. Passing a certain building, a particular tree, a church with a tall spire, can cause anxiety to build up. Even the lighting in a famous chain of shops for some reason is an anxiety-provoking factor. A person who is mildly agoraphobic, perhaps without even realizing it, may unconsciously plot a route to avoid 'hostile' spots and steer an erratic course between her home and her destination, crossing to one side of the road at one point, then back again further on.

In their normal everyday lives there was no reason for some of these patients to travel on tube trains or rush around city centres. In therapy they were learning to cope with such situations, but so often their problem lay much nearer home – the place where the phobic habit had been established.

The agoraphobe is afraid of the physical feelings she experiences in certain situations and she must be taught to cope with these feelings – *not the situation*. Otherwise, even though she learns to deal with a number of her dreaded spots, she will be likely to panic when in a new one.

There is no one 'cure' for agoraphobia; each patient has a different set of symptoms, a different set of problems. Each needs a course of treatment planned for her alone; drugs may be necessary, but behaviour therapy in some form is the way to recovery.

No treatment available to you? Do not despair; it *is* possible to tackle the problem on your own, as we shall see in a later chapter.

CHAPTER 6

Could this be the Answer? (OBD)

'He that is giddy thinks the world turns round.'
Shakespeare, *Love's Labour's Lost*

Did you crawl when you were a young child? Perhaps you took your first tottering steps at an early age, to the delight of your parents who felt you were more advanced than the creeping, grubby-kneed babies of their friends. Do you kick a ball with your right foot, but catch it in your left hand? These questions may appear to have little to do with agoraphobia, but psychologists Peter Blythe and David McGlown at the Institute for Neuro-Physiological Psychology in Chester have discovered that many agoraphobia sufferers have definite physical characteristics which could, under certain conditions, be a cause of anxiety and panic attacks.

We are all born with a number of infant survival reflexes which are controlled by the brain during the first months of life, after which time they are gradually replaced by appropriate adult reflexes. The babies of our primitive ancestors had to cling tightly as their mother swung through the trees or fled from danger – a reflex that was vital for their survival. Today's newborn will still grip firmly to a proffered finger and hang on tightly while being lifted.

Babies can swim when only a few weeks old. If placed in the water in a prone position, they do not struggle but make reflex swimming movements which actually propel them forward. However, by the time they are four months old, they have lost this automatic swimming response; they rotate into a supine position, struggle and clutch at adult hands for support.

Thousands of years ago these and other reflexes were necessary if the baby was to survive and they still exist in each child today until such time as they are no longer necessary. Some of us, for one reason or another, retain as adults certain infant survival reflexes which should have been controlled by the brain before we were two years old.

Sometimes a difficult birth, a feverish illness such as measles or whooping-cough can result in a weakened central nervous system caused by brain dysfunction. Many children are affected in this way and it should not be confused with brain damage, but seen rather as a difficulty in controlling functions. Blythe and McGlown refer to this condition as OBD, organic brain dysfunction, and believe that it is the cause of adult reflexes not developing to take the place of the infant reflexes.

Brain dysfunction . . . a weakened central nervous system – diagnoses which will give a real nervous jolt to many agoraphobes reading this book, but fear not! OBD is not some terrible disability which is going to cripple you; in fact the majority of those with OBD are not affected by it at all, since their brain will compensate. In some cases, however, the brain compensation will be too much to cope with and the person will be prone to anxiety and other problems.

Ruth Hurst Vose, in her book *Agoraphobia*, writes:

> Put very simply, if the reflexes of childhood are not transformed into adult reflexes which are necessary for our proper functions as an adult, we are going to be in trouble both emotionally and physically. It has been found that if more than two primitive

reflexes are still with us as adults we are much more prone to stress and the disorders this brings.

It is a relief to know that not only can OBD be detected but the amount of dysfunction can be measured and, most important, corrected.

In the early years of this century Sigmund Freud said he believed that one day someone would find a physical basis for neurosis. Recently, Professor Isaac Marks wrote: 'We are left with the question of the origin of the general anxiety in agoraphobics. No one has yet answered this adequately.'

This statement was taken up by Dr Claire Weekes who said: '. . . In my opinion to put agoraphobia in the first place and general anxiety in the second is to reverse their true order. The majority of my patients first developed an anxiety state from which agoraphobia arose as a secondary phase.'

It is accepted that all anxiety states are accompanied by some degree of physical sensation and discomfort caused by an upset of the nervous system. The anxiety triggers off a stress reaction in the body, causing the unpleasant symptoms the agoraphobic sufferer recognizes only too well. This has resulted in many doctors telling agoraphobic patients that all their experienced symptoms are the result of their anxiety state.

ANXIETY CAN CAUSE UNPLEASANT PHYSICAL SYMPTOMS
UNPLEASANT PHYSICAL SYMPTOMS CAN CAUSE ANXIETY

Which comes first?

Blythe and McGlown define two different types of agoraphobia. The first is the psychological type where there is a definite phobic fear that something terrible is going to happen – a calamity syndrome. These purely emotional agoraphobia sufferers form about 25–30 per cent of the agoraphobic population; generally speaking, since their condition is due to emotional factors and learned behaviour when the patient is frightened to go out, it will respond to whichever therapy they find most helpful.

The remaining 70–75 per cent of agoraphobic and anxiety sufferers have some degree of OBD which makes them prone to stress symptoms. When under pressure, they find that their eyes play tricks and their balancing mechanism is upset, making them feel dizzy and unsafe. Their continued effort to keep control increases the internal stress level, resulting in emotional distress.

A link between a dysfunction in the balancing mechanism and resulting anxiety was made by Feldenkrais (1949) when he described dizziness as being connected with a disorder of the balancing mechanism which frightened the sufferer and caused pallor, nausea, vomiting and breathing and pulse alterations.

In a paper by Woolfson, Marlowe, Silverstein and Keels (1981), the authors made a statement which is relevant to agoraphobia: 'Patients are often emotionally upset after an episode of vertigo and especially when it develops without warning, they may become extremely frightened . . .'

The important point about this statement is that most agoraphobes complain of either objective vertigo – when the person feels as if she is stationary and the objects seem to move around her – or subjective vertigo, when she feels as if she is turning in a stationary environment. Because the majority experience their first attack of vertigo without any warning whatsoever, they quickly develop a 'neurotic' fear of it happening again.

Peter Blythe explains that man is a biped animal dependent upon his balancing mechanism to keep his upright position in space:

If he suffers from 'gravitational insecurity' because his balancing mechanism is not functioning properly, the lack of balance and resulting feeling of insecurity gives rise to anxiety; stress

Perceptual problems

hormones are released, causing even greater internal excitation and anxiety . . .

Agoraphobes with OBD problems are generally found to be 'stimulus bound', which means they are unable to ignore irrelevant movements going on around them. Disturbed by too much action and too many people moving in their field of vision, and becoming overwhelmed by a barrage of stimuli, they feel that they are going to fall over or faint. Most agoraphobes will describe these sensations and we begin to see why 'fear of the market place' is not such a bad description of the problem. The agoraphobic sufferers who prefer to go out after dark or who feel 'safer' when wearing dark glasses are subconsciously trying to cut down on the disturbing stimulus of sound and noise that is going on around them. 'Where there is a concentration of irregular movement, noise and bright light,' says Ruth Hurst Vose, 'the stimulus can get too much and the central nervous system will "blow a fuse".'

Some years ago, a TOD member described an outing with a nurse-therapist and four other patients. Her agoraphobia had improved and she had not experienced a panic attack for several months. On this occasion it was decided that the group would make a journey on the Underground:

The prospect of plunging into the bowels of the earth did not bother me, strangely enough. I coped with the escalator, though the movement had always upset me before as I felt so unsafe and wobbly. The lighting was a slight problem and the others in the group laughed at me when I put my dark glasses on (they are one of my 'Aggie-props'). It was when I heard the train coming that I knew I was in for trouble, but I gritted my teeth and got in. The doors closed and then as the train started the awful noise began to build up. The movement and the sound made my head spin and I thought my ears would burst; I tried to keep myself under control as I didn't want to upset the others, who I knew might react badly, but I had the sort of acute panic I had not experienced for months and when we got out at the next stop I had to sit on a seat on the platform and gasp for breath. I knew I was over-breathing which made things worse and the sound of another train approaching was the final straw. I fled for the escalator and kept going until I got outside into the open air. I was afraid this was going to be a real setback, but once I had realized that never never again would there be any necessity for me to go on the tube I felt happier and continued to make progress.

Another member suffered from what everyone, himself included, considered a 'dental phobia'. He found it difficult to understand, as he had never had any traumatic experiences while undergoing dental treatment, but suddenly realized that it was the chair which was the problem. As soon as he was tilted backwards he felt insecure and dizzy, with the usual anxiety feelings building up. With the help of an interested and understanding dentist he gradually overcame the anxiety, receiving treatment while sitting upright on a dining-room chair, then gradually accustoming himself to tolerating the angle of the surgery chair.

Another person with balancing and perceptual problems was a twelve-year-old boy whose mother wrote:

Neil had been having problems with school phobia and we had reached the stage where he was refusing to go to school at all. The school doctor was very helpful and after much questioning decided that the problem lay in PE lessons. . . . Neil has always been rather uncoordinated, but he denied that there was any teasing from other boys about his clumsiness . . . we found that his real dread was having to do handstands, 'forward rolls' and hanging upside-down from the wall bars. We realized that much of his problem might have a physical foundation, though a full medical examination showed that he was in good health and his eyesight normal. The PE instructor and school doctor between them devised a sort of remedial programme and twice a week Neil has special lessons on his own in which he is taught gradually to do certain exercises until he can cope with the feelings of disorientation associated with being upside-down. He now only participates in the class exercises when he wants to – the explanation to the other boys is that he has ear problems. The change in him is remarkable . . . it is frightening to realise that such a relatively minor problem can have such a drastic effect on a child's wellbeing . . .

Each person in the above examples may well have had OBD problems with which they were able unconsciously to come to terms. It seems significant that discovering the cause of their anxiety helped them to overcome their fears of specific situations.

People with brain dysfunction may have problems with spatial orientation – experiencing difficulties in distinguishing left from right and having no sense of direction when they attempt to read a map or to navigate whilst driving (Bellak, 1979):

Failure to establish clear boundaries in turn has an effect on object relations, leading to insufficient individualization and a poorly defined self-image. Typically both children and adults with minimal brain dysfunction feel perplexed, and others suffer from the uncomfortable sensation of being lost, which may at times produce high levels of anxiety.

The Chester Institute for Neuro-Physiological Psychology will carry out extensive tests for dysfunction in a patient and can also measure the percentage of dysfunction, correcting it with a programme of simple remedial exercises tailored to the individual. The patient is also screened to establish that the problems are due to basic organic faults and not purely emotional.

If the emotional screening shows that the agoraphobia

has a psychological foundation, the appropriate therapy can be worked out by the Institute.

Certain apparently unrelated questions do help to pinpoint which part of the nervous system is weakened. See if any of these might apply in your case.

1 Did you have problems at school while in the gym?

2 Did you suffer from travel sickness as a child?

3 During school assembly, did you occasionally have the fear that you would faint or fall over?

4 When you are very tired, do you lose coordination and become clumsy? Do you drop things, miss the door handle etc?

5 Do you become anxious if there are too many people moving about around you, or if too many people talk at the same time?

6 When very tired, do you find that you know what you want to say, but what you actually say is not what you intend?

7 Do you have difficulty in differentiating between left and right?

The Institute has found that if the agoraphobe who has lost the ability to compensate for underlying organic brain dysfunction is put on to a remedial programme of exercises – and does them regularly in their own home – the prospect of success is very good.

In her book, Ruth Hurst Vose describes how agoraphobia wrecked her professional and private life until after two and a half years of psychoanalysis and hypnotherapy she had improved 'beyond all hope'; she then decided to try to speed up her recovery by undergoing a series of tests at the Institute, to see if there were any physical, neurological or emotional impediments to her recovery which were as yet undetected:

Not only had the personality tests revealed my character precisely and most uncomfortably (David McGlown had never met me before the tests), but there was also neurological evidence of minimal or organic brain dysfunction – difficulties of functioning caused by small faults within the central nervous system. My gross muscle coordination was not very good, and I had such problems with eye muscle movement that to focus my eyes on an object cost me a great deal more effort than for people with normal eyes . . .

The effect of the first exercise programme was immediate. I had unconsciously been using my left eye for sighting when doing close work, but on the first day of wearing the eye-patch, which took the stress off my eye muscles and forced me to focus with my right eye, my temper improved dramatically. Within a short time I found I could work for longer periods without getting tired and the feelings of unreality and depersonalisation slowly diminished.

Psychotherapy helped Ruth to speed up her recovery as she 'galloped through a series of emotional explosions', clearing the psychological problems which she realized had appeared largely as a result of her brain dysfunctions. Having made a complete recovery, Ruth has been able to resume her professional life as a writer, lecturer and publicity consultant.

Another patient successfully treated by Blythe and McGlown is John, a high-powered businessman and lecturer who had been suffering from agoraphobia for twenty-five years since adolescence. Within six weeks of starting treatment, the perceptual problems which had caused him to see distorted images had disappeared; other dysfunctions had also been corrected and John was able to fly around the world on a business trip, euphoric with the new feeling of freedom that he was experiencing.

Looking back over forty years to when my anxiety state was affecting my school life, I can see so many indications that I must have had OBD problems. I was and am completely ambidextrous – cross-laterality has been associated with a vulnerability to physical stress. I never crawled – a child who has not developed a transformed tonic neck reflex will never go through the stages of crawling and will have lost out on a vital stage in neural development. Turning my head suddenly to the left or looking upwards made me feel 'odd', while being blindfolded produced feelings of acute disorientation – visual perceptual problems which are to do not with sight, but with how the eye muscles work and the signals the eyes send back to the visual cortex of the brain.

The Chester Institute has found that in 30–50 per cent of the patients with OBD, there appears to be an hereditary factor. My mother, who was also agoraphobic for many years, has exactly the same physical idiosyncrasies as I have; the fact that we each fought our way through agoraphobia to emerge as well-balanced individuals with particularly steady nerves was partly good luck but mostly hard work and a determination to recover. I am personally convinced that Peter Blythe and David McGlown are working in the right direction in finding a cause and cure for the background problems of agoraphobia.

Of course, when the physical abnormalities have been corrected there will still be the habit of agoraphobia to deal with, but without these background problems cracking the habit should be much easier.

CHAPTER 7

A Breath of Fresh Air

'I pant, I sink, I tremble, I expire!'

Shelley

When a wild animal scents danger, for a second or so it freezes in its tracks and stays perfectly still, wide-eyed and alert, holding its breath as though any sound of breathing or sense of the muscular movements which control the breathing will affect its concentration. Then the tension suddenly snaps and the creature leaps in the direction of safety.

We may catch our breath if we have a narrow escape; in a dangerous situation we behave like the animal, for fear is experienced and the reaction is immediate. Holding the breath is a normal response when we are suddenly surprised or in some kind of danger; a response which is usually corrected automatically as we gasp with relief and inhale deeply, filling our lungs with air. But for the agoraphobic sufferer this does not always happen; her nervous system has been permanently conditioned to react to dangers that exist only in her mind, and her body responds by remaining constantly on the alert with muscles tense and breathing fast and shallow.

Frederick Perls, author of *Gestalt Therapy*, describes anxiety as '*the experience of breathing difficulty during any blocked excitement.* It is the experience of trying to get more air into lungs immobilized by muscular constriction of the thoracic cage.'

Perls defines excitement as the heightened mobilization of energy which occurs 'whenever there is strong concern and strong contact, whether erotic, aggressive or whatever.' The average person reacts to excitement by increasing the rate and amplitude of their breathing; the chronically anxious agoraphobe, on the other hand, attempts to control her emotions by interfering with her breathing, deliberately trying to appear calm and controlled and hiding her natural urge to pant and gasp as she takes shallow breaths and blocks off her oxygen supply. During a panic attack she may fold her arms or clasp her hands across her diaphragm – literally 'pulling herself together' – as she struggles for control. This posture accentuates the automatic constriction of the chest when it is deprived of oxygen. The agoraphobe cannot exhale and inhale properly; in other words she simply cannot breathe correctly, and she is not aware of what she is doing as she tenses all the wrong muscles in the desperate attempt to appear normal.

No gasp, sob or call for help will pass the agoraphobe's lips if she can possibly help it. 'How dreadful it would be to expose your weakness and your emotions,' she thinks. A person without anxiety problems, without the same need to display a brave front in a dodgy situation, will allow herself to let out a yell of fright and her breathing will quickly return to normal when the cause of fear has disappeared.

The following passage was written by a 17-year-old schoolgirl who for most of the time was coping well with her agoraphobia:

I was standing at a bus stop when a woman ran across the road in front of me and was knocked down by a car. She let out an awful shriek and was hurled on to the pavement. I held my breath with fright and was rooted to the spot as people ran to help her. The dreadful part was that I could not get my breath back and had the most terrible feeling of panic. I was taking whistling in-breaths and thought I would faint ... A girl standing next to me put her arm around my shoulder and tried to help me to calm down. The silly thing was that the woman who had been knocked down was only bruised – she picked herself up and came over to see how *I* was! I can't tell you how ashamed I felt. I now have to avoid that bus stop in case I might bump into anyone who saw me that day.

It happens only too often that the anticipation of a future event can cause a build-up of anxiety which will inevitably result in changes in the breathing pattern. To be 'breathless with excitement' is a pleasant state for many people, but for the agoraphobe it just means that even the happiest occasion can be spoiled by acute anxiety and accompanying distress, anxiety caused by deliberately blocking excitement.

I should be looking forward to my daughter's wedding, but know the old Aggie problem will inevitably raise its ugly head. Why *can't* I enjoy such a joyful day instead of dreading it so much? Why should it be spoiled by the panic attack that will probably sweep over me, or at best, hours of distress which I will have to struggle to hide so I don't spoil the day for the rest of the family.

Members of the acting profession are taught how to breathe correctly in order to be able to project their voices and also to combat the thrills of the build-up before a performance, when incorrect breathing would cause anxiety which could escalate into acute and even disabling stage fright. Breathing properly allows the excitement to be properly expressed; the performance then becomes enjoyable instead of being a dreadful ordeal.

It is well understood in the families of severe agoraphobes that one must not upset the sufferer, since violent arguments or outbursts of anger are likely to provoke an anxiety attack. Bad temper or a sudden shock will cause the sufferer to 'over-control' and start to breathe rapidly and wrongly.

My mother was agoraphobic for two years and as children we learned never to shout, 'Mummy, come quickly!' or to squabble between ourselves. As for screaming – we were in dead trouble, as any upset would cause her to have an anxiety attack.

Breathing is not just inhaling; it is the full cycle of exhaling and inhaling. Normally, breathing out does not require any effort, since it just means letting go and allowing the muscles which lift the ribs and lower the diaphragm to relax. When the lungs are emptied fresh air can then enter, but the amount of fresh air which can be inhaled depends upon how much has been exhaled, so you will see that breathing out properly is more important than breathing in. Here are a few expert comments on this:

> I ask the patient to see how long he can hold his breath. At first he may be reluctant to try such a dangerous experiment but when he does he is surprised to find that after about half a minute he is able to take a very deep breath indeed.
>
> Dr Claire Weekes, *Agoraphobia*

> If you feel that you can't catch your breath or breathe deeply, try this: Take a deep breath and hold it as long as you possibly can until you feel you are absolutely bursting. Don't cheat by taking little breaths. Time yourself. You will find that in about sixty seconds you simply can't keep from breathing any longer. Your body's reflexes will force you to take a deep breath.
>
> Isaac Marks, *Living With Fear*

> Partial relief of any given instance of anxiety can be obtained, paradoxically, by tightening even further the narrowness of the chest instead of resisting it. In other words you give in and go along with the motor impulse that you feel.
>
> Frederick Perls, *Gestalt Therapy*

Perls advises that you deliberately squeeze your chest as tightly as you possibly can, until you have pushed every ounce of breath out of your lungs. This results in a great healing draught of fresh air as you thankfully inhale.

Everyone knows that the body needs oxygen in order to stay alive, but the rate and depth of breathing controlled by the respiratory centre in the brain is affected not by a lack of oxygen, but in the concentration of carbon dioxide in the blood. If we over-breathe and take in more air than our body needs, too much carbon dioxide is 'washed' out of the blood, resulting in dizziness, tingling in the fingers and other unpleasant sensations. Both Professor Marks and Dr Weekes advise carrying a paper or plastic bag around with you; when you find anxiety building up because of your erratic breathing, seek a quiet corner and put the bag over your mouth, breathing in and out several times so that you re-inhale the carbon dioxide you have just exhaled.

Over-breathing can be catching

Professor Marks describes how epidemics of mass hysteria with acute anxiety, over-breathing and faintness sometimes occur in groups of young women. I experienced this phenomenon myself when at the age of fourteen I was at boarding school. It was wartime in 1944, and we had a memorial service in the school chapel on the anniversay of Armistice Day. During a very emotional hymn – 'Oh valiant hearts, to whom your glory came . . .' – one of the girls threw a dramatic swoon and was quickly followed by another and another until the chapel was full of sobbing and fainting girls, who in a state of emotional excitement were all over-breathing like mad and passing out from the results of so doing.

Me? Knowing that one of my 'funny turns' was coming

Mass hysteria

on, I had scuttled out of chapel and was half-way across the playing field before the drama took place. The following Armistice Day, 'Valiant Hearts' was banned and the choir sang, 'O Lovely Peace' instead.

How do we know when we are breathing incorrectly and what can we do to combat this? Jane Madders, author of *Stress and Relaxation*, explains:

> The kind of breathing associated with anxiety is mainly in the upper chest. You can observe this in the way the collar or neckline moves up and down markedly at each breath and the rate of breathing is fast. In contrast, slow breathing, using the lower part of the lungs, with the emphasis on the outbreath, is a help in general relaxation and in relieving the symptoms of over-breathing . . .

The following exercises and comments from Jane Madders' book are reproduced here with her kind permission:

Breathing, muscle tension and relaxation

There is a useful link between breathing and relaxation. Try this: tighten up all your muscles as hard as you can . . . very tight . . . then tighter. Then let go and relax. You probably found that, as you tightened up, you held your breath and as you relaxed you let it go. This link between the outbreath and relaxation is a useful one and can be used whenever you practise (there will be no need again to tighten up first).

You may also have noticed that your abdominal muscles contracted in the way they do whenever you are anxious or alert. This exercise therefore combines calm breathing with the relaxation of abdominal muscles.

Put one hand on the upper part of your chest and the other on top of your abdomen (on top of the bulge if you have one). Exhale first, then inhale comfortably. If you are doing this correctly your abdomen rises at the start of the breath, but if your chest moved first this is an inefficient kind of breathing.

Do it again several times and try to breathe so that there is very little movement in the upper chest but plenty under your lower hand. Later on you will find that your back is also involved in breathing and your lower ribs spread sideways. Don't bother much about this. Every time you breathe out do it *slowly* with a slight sigh, rather like a balloon gently deflating. After exhaling, pause a moment and let the breath come in just as much as the body wants; don't exaggerate the breathing in, let it happen. Combine the outbreath with relaxation whenever you practise. Two or three of these calm breaths are enough at the beginning of relaxation practice. In deep relaxation you will find that the body requires less oxygen and less carbon dioxide is produced so the breathing becomes shallow, slow and gentle.

Knowing how to combat your anxiety in a positive way will enable you to tackle your agoraphobic hurdles with an increasing sense of confidence – and don't forget your 'breathing bag'!

CHAPTER 8

Alternative Therapies

'Help! I need somebody.'

Beatles

There are many roads to explore on the way to recovery and there is no doubt that some agoraphobia sufferers – unhappy with conventional treatment, or lack of treatment – have made some progress when changing direction. Cynics will say that the patient was probably on the point of recovery in any case and the fact that a different approach appeared to be successful just happened to be a happy coincidence. Many TOD members were enthusiastic about trying anything which might improve their emotional and physical state and help them to tackle the agoraphobic problem in a more positive way.

Of course alternative medicine offers literally hundreds of different therapies and remedies, but here we will consider only those which have been tried by people seeking relief from agoraphobic and anxiety symptoms.

Hypnosis

The Greeks used hypnosis as a form of therapy for anxiety and hysterical states; the ancient Druids called it 'magic sleep' and used it to cure warts and cast spells. Before Franz Anton Mesmer employed the technique on his patients, the word 'hypnosis' (from the Greek word *hypnos* – sleep) was coined by James Braid, a nineteenth-century surgeon who used it for major surgery.

The Druids used hypnosis

Because Mesmer employed a theatrical approach and his public demonstrations with susceptible subjects caused them to make fools of themselves to the amusement of an audience, hypnosis acquired a bad name and has been regarded with some suspicion until fairly recently. The medical profession was very cynical; Dr John Elliotson, who hypnotized patients instead of filling their lungs with the poisonous chemical anaesthetics of the day, was attacked by his colleagues who accused him of having bribed his patients not to scream while he operated.

Hypnosis is not sleep. Many people can be hypnotized

and remain wide awake and conscious of their surroundings, and it is quite possible for the subjects to resist and reject ideas and suggestions made to them by the hypnotist. Though hypnosis can be helpful in achieving a state of complete relaxation, it is difficult to hypnotize someone who is excessively anxious – the type of person who needs to relax most of all.

A TOD member described her experiences after a friend had recommended her own hypnotherapist who had proved very helpful. She was apprehensive because she had a dread of anaesthetics and felt that hypnosis might have a similar effect – that she would not be in control of her own body and mind. After the first two sessions, she wrote to the TOD newsletter to describe her experiences:

> During the first session, she (the hypnotherapist) took my case history and we discussed whether there might be any deeper causes for my agoraphobia. I told her about my fears and my anaesthetic phobia and she was very reassuring, explaining that there was nothing for me to worry about . . . I was then tested to find out if I would respond to hypnosis. I was told that my eyes were becoming tired and beginning to close and then she asked me to concentrate on the hand I used least. As she told me my hand was getting lighter and rising up I realised that was exactly what was happening, after which I was told to relax deeper and deeper.
>
> My next visit found me much less nervous. The hypnotherapist asked me to lie down, breathe deeply and think of a time and place when I had felt tranquil and happy. Again I became more and more relaxed and was told at the end of the session that I had actually been in a light trance. I must admit I was a little disappointed when told not to expect my symptoms to disappear as a result of hypnosis, but now realise that it can help me gain confidence to tackle the agoraphobia problems.

Another woman had been agoraphobic for eight years, during four years of which she had been virtually housebound. Psychiatric treatment and drugs had helped a little, but she felt that progress should be faster and was lucky enough to find a psychiatrist who also practised hypnosis at her local NHS hospital:

I didn't get put to sleep and feel wonderful as I had been led to believe though I can't say the experience was unpleasant. But next morning I felt marvellous – like I hadn't felt for years. I could hardly believe it. I felt like this for three days and did all sorts of things I hadn't done for ages . . . then the effect wore off and I was back where I started until I went for treatment number two.

My second appointment was at a bad time; I had sinus trouble and was feeling really low. But I went and again I benefited. Could this really be me throwing 'Aggie' off so easily?

On my third visit the hypnotherapist took me through a panic. He put me under hypnosis and when I was completely relaxed told me I was now getting into a panic. He kept telling me that the panic was getting worse, while I had to imagine I was in the supermarket. Then when I felt I would get up and run out, he said he would count to ten and the panic would get worse and worse. At ten I thought I'd go really mad but he then calmed me down, still in the supermarket situation. He made me feel really calm, then woke me up. My goodness, was I exhausted! However I got up slowly and came out feeling on top of the world and was able to go out with my husband for the rest of the evening.

It was now a regular thing to feel completely free of 'Aggie' for three days after treatment, but after session three on day four I suddenly became very weepy and stayed like this until my next appointment. My psychiatrist assured me that this was a normal side-effect of hypnosis for someone like myself who had repressed my feelings for years. Having hypnosis opens up the subconscious mind and things that have been buried in the past come floating to the surface. He explained that it was good for me to be weepy as my emotions were being liberated.

The next time I had treatment I was even more weepy for a day but as the week wore on I began to feel better. After the fifth session I began to notice how much more relaxed I was generally and was able to go into crowded places. On Easter Sunday morning I went to church. That really was a big step forward; it was also the first Bank Holiday I can remember ever going out and enjoying myself. I could hardly believe that five ten-minute sessions of hypnosis had made such a difference to my life.

Since Easter I have had three more sessions. My only fear now is that the effects may not last, but I am assured that because I have learnt to relax and my confidence has increased a hundred per cent that I could cope with panic if it does arise again.

Jean (34) mother of two.

Hypnosis is sometimes used in desensitization therapy to produce a state of relaxation, but without desensitization it will rarely have a lasting effect in overcoming fear unless the patient is taught how to cope with panic. Agoraphobes who hope to be told that their fears will just melt away will be disappointed when they find there is still a lot of hard work to be done.

Unfortunately, it is the hope of an easy cure which causes agoraphobes and those suffering from anxiety states to put themselves at risk in the hands of unqualified practitioners. There are many lay therapists who are excellent and have been extremely helpful to phobic sufferers, but it is a good rule – if you are proposing to consult one of these therapists – to do so only on the recommendation of another patient who has had experience of their technique. Alternatively, of course, you can get in touch with the British Society of Dental and Medical Hypnosis or the Association of Hypnotists and Psychotherapists, who keep registers of practitioners. Hypnotherapy is becoming more readily available in NHS hospitals and, as stated before, is used in conjunction with other therapies such as desensitization.

Acupuncture

The word acupuncture comes from the Latin words *acus* (needle) and *punctura* (to prick). It is used to describe a technique in which needles are used to puncture the skin at certain defined points in order to restore the balance of energy which acupuncturists believe is essential to good health.

In the West we look on the body as a piece of machinery which needs constant maintenance and repair. When something goes wrong, we rush it into the workshop (doctor's surgery) to be fitted with spare parts: fuel, lubricants and various nuts and bolts which will enable it to keep going until another bit needs attention. To the ancient Chinese, the human being was a living thing, not just a machine but 'a field for the action and interaction of the invisible forces of life'. Dr Felix Mann, author of *Acupuncture, Cure of many Diseases* also points out:

> The harmony of these vital powers within was revealed by the health of the whole body, their disharmony by disease, their disappearance by its death. So the aim of the Chinese doctor was to correct the imbalance of the vital forces in the body. Once the harmonious interplay of these forces had been resolved the patient himself was able to overcome his weakness.

The flow of nervous energy through the body was described by the Chinese as *chi* – the energy of life; something like a wave of electricity running along the nerve. They called the principal nerve endings acupuncture points and in Chinese literature there are descriptions of about a thousand such points classified into twelve main groups. All the points in any one of these groups are joined by a line which is known as a meridian. *Chi* was regarded as a river which flowed through the meridians. If the body was diseased or disturbed, a blockage occurred and the flow of *chi* slowed down. The acupuncture needle would remove the blockage, opening up the channel so that once more *chi* was able to flow through it.

Most people who have nervous problems are considered to have some underactivity of the kidneys. If you consider this, you will realize that one of the symptoms of fear is a need to urinate. In these cases the acupuncturist would treat the points on the kidney meridian which runs down the lower parts of the arms and legs. The needles would be inserted and, during the ten minutes or so while they are left in place, they may be twirled from time to time by the therapist in order to increase the flow of *chi*. During this time the patient might feel a slight tingling sensation – a positive feeling, proving that the system was being 'tuned up'.

I have had a number of enthusiastic reports from acupunctured agoraphobes:

> I was so nervous when I went for my first session and even more so when the doctor told me that he could not cure my agoraphobia. That was the whole reason for my consulting him and I was almost ready to abandon the whole thing. There was a slight tingling in my forearms and down my legs and I immediately felt much better – for some reason I had expected the needles to be put in my head! I think that was the main reason for my apprehension beforehand. The needles were left in place for about ten minutes after which time I felt relaxed and rested – though a bit disconcerted to find that for several hours after the treatment I felt 'electric shocks' in my legs.
>
> I have been regularly for treatment for six months and my anxiety state is greatly improved. The agoraphobia bit I am

tackling with a programme drawn up with the doctor. We discuss my progress before each treatment session and when I am relaxed and doing my pincushion act we plan the next part of my programme and the obstacles I propose to tackle.

I really feel that acupuncture is working for me particularly as the doctor understands the agoraphobia condition so well.

Acupuncture does not depend solely on correct diagnosis and accurate positioning of needles during treatment, with the patient as passive onlooker while everything is done for her. With the anxiety damped down, there is still a lot of hard work to do.

Shiatsu and Acupressure

Acupressure is a form of acupuncture without needles – literally, 'finger pressure'. Shiatsu is the Japanese form of this, though during treatment pressure can be applied not only by the fingers and thumbs but by the palm or heel of the hand, a knee, an elbow or the feet.

In Japan, Shiatsu has always been a kind of family therapy, a remedial massage performed by one member of the family on another. The pressure is designed to stimulate the acupuncture points and meridians, to alter the energy flow in the body either to sedate them or tone them up.

A good Shiatsu practitioner can make the patient feel elated or sedated, depending on what he does and which meridians he stimulates. This therapy is particularly suitable for a nervous patient who may be worried about needles.

A form of acupressure massage which anyone can use on themselves is known as 'Do-in'. When the subject has learned the basic acupuncture points, she can work along the meridians or just concentrate on the parts which appear to bring relief from symptoms. There are many books which have instructions on do-it-yourself acupressure, and recently available are tiny magnets which are fixed over the acupuncture points with adhesive plasters, the idea being that they provide a constant pressure and can also be pressed more firmly from time to time in order to increase the energy flow through the meridians.

Yoga

Yoga is chiefly concerned with exercises designed to improve posture and breathing, on the principle that these lead not only to better physical health but also to greater self-confidence and serenity because stress and tension are removed. The yoga postures range from sitting positions to movements aimed at toning the body and making it supple. Each posture has three main parts – a bodily movement, a mental control process and a specific control of respiration. Great emphasis is put on correct breathing.

As we know, agoraphobes are tense and inclined to breathe in a shallow and irregular way, so a yoga instructor will start off by getting the subject to breathe correctly. When the body is calm and relaxed, the life forces are more in harmony.

I have to admit that TOD members who have managed to get to yoga classes may not always have appreciated the deeper meanings behind the movements, but have certainly benefited from the social side of the sessions. On the whole yoga proved helpful in a number of ways and one TOD lady eventually became a yoga instructress herself.

It is not advisable to try 'do-it-yourself' yoga unless you have attended classes in the first place.

Healing

I had not met the minister before he came to my house that evening. I had heard that other people suffering from nervous illness had been helped by him and though I had been house-bound for three years I just had the feeling that this man would be my salvation. When he sat down and took my hands in his I burst into tears. For half an hour the minister sat with me, praying for my recovery, and gradually I became more and more certain that I *would* get better.

Next day I went out with my daughter. Not just to the front gate or to the corner of the road, but right round the block. I kept saying, 'I'm not afraid any more, I know I can do it.' I now go out *every day* much to the delight of my family. Flashes of memory of the old terrors sometimes disturb me but I put them to the back of my mind and tell myself that everyone feels a little peculiar at times and I am just as normal as anyone else.

I feel that God meant me to get better at that moment. He showed me what it was like to be able to go out and enjoy the world and I could not let him down by ever backsliding.

Beryl (60)

In many cultures it is accepted that the laying on of hands can effect a healing process. Healing simply makes use of a kind of empathy as the main source of healing power, though many hand healers now assume that there is some bio-electromagnetic element in healing.

Basically there are two kinds of healer. The spiritual healer works on the principle that whatever one believes can be made to happen – helping the patient to 'tune-in' to his God, Life Force or Higher Power or whatever he believes in. Once this happens, he is open to receive the healing force.

Spirit healing includes contact with the world of disincarnate spirits through clairvoyants, spiritualists and other psychics. There are many charlatans in this group and I hesitate to suggest that agoraphobes dabble in this field, because a bad experience might upset an already over-sensitized nervous system and thus cause a great deal of distress. I cannot deny, however, that I have known people to make a spectacular recovery after consulting a psychic healer.

The most famous healer in Britain in recent times was Harry Edwards. He claimed that all forms of spiritual healing come from God and that healers are obeying Jesus' order, also from God, to heal the sick. They do not themselves possess healing powers, but are the instruments through whom the divine plan is carried out. Healers are chosen because they have the capacity to channel the healing force through themselves into other people. When a healing occurs, therefore, it is not an indication of divine favour; it is simply a further proof that such healing is available to all and sundry, given the individual's desire to *be* healed.

> I was determined to go to the meeting as I had heard that this healer had performed unbelievable miracles for other people like myself who had suffered from nerves for most of my adult life. My husband took me, although he was very sceptical and I think he was afraid that I would be so disappointed I would just give up completely. I had to have a chair by the open door at the back of the hall – difficult because there were so many people grouped around there and somebody made a joke about claustrophobia.
>
> What happened is a bit of a blur. I found the whole thing so emotional I couldn't stop crying . . . I had thought that people would have to go up on to the stage to him, but he came down to the audience, sat with different people and talked to them and stroked their head. There was no excited hysteria as I had expected, just a sort of quiet joy, as people stood, walked, flexed muscles that had been locked. I just wish I had been able to have a clear picture instead of sitting and crying and so wrapped up in myself. When he came to me I managed to stop crying and whispered that I had been suffering from agoraphobia for so

many years I was afraid I would never get better. He put his hands on my shoulders and looked into my eyes and said, 'God wants you to get better, if *you* want to get better you will.' 'At least you've stopped her crying,' said my husband.

I find I am more relaxed and have a wonderful feeling of peace these days. I haven't managed to do anything very spectacular, but I know it is only a matter of time before I can do all the things I have missed over the 'Aggie' years. If I happen to feel a bit down I say to myself, 'God wants me to get better – I want to get better.'

Margaret (43), married, no children.

Homoeopathy

Wherever she goes, the Queen takes a battered black box full of medicines many chemists have never heard of . . .

The Queen . . . uses arsenic for sneezing, or an upset stomach, onion for a runny nose, and anemone when someone is down in the dumps after an illness . . .

The Queen's interest in homoeopathy – a system of 'alternative' medicine developed at the end of the eighteenth century – stems from childhood. Her father, the late King George VI, used to treat both his daughters this way.

James Whitaker, London *Daily Star*, 1st February 1980.

Homoeopathy is based on the principle that a disease does not attack the body but rather is the body's method of curing itself of something which is wrong. Samuel Hahnemann, a German doctor in the early nineteenth century, believed that any substance which actually induces symptoms similar to those of a particular disease is probably stimulating the disease-fighting systems in the body and so is able to cure the condition. Hahnemann taught that the smaller the potency of the drug administered, the more easily it is absorbed into the sick body which would reject a stronger dose. The substances from which the homoeopathic drugs are obtained would in many cases be exceedingly poisonous if taken in anything but minute quantities. In the dilute form in which they are administered, they are absolutely safe.

This form of medicine is available under the National Health Service and the Faculty of Homoeopathy in London is recognized in law just like all the other medical faculties. Any general practitioner can write a prescription for a homoeopathic patient and many chemists stock homoeopathic medicines. There are also lay homoeopaths practising in this country who are not qualified doctors but may be osteopaths, acupuncturists or other practitioners of alternative medicine who use homoeopathic remedies in conjunction with their own specific type of therapy.

Homoeopathy is 'whole person' medicine. During the initial consultation a homoeopathic doctor will note down a detailed history, taking into account the patient's lifestyle, personality, temperament and even general likes and dislikes. He will not concentrate on symptoms alone, because two patients with exactly similar symptoms may need to be treated very differently.

Homoeopathic remedies are widely available and 'first aid kits' can be purchased in chemists' shops. They are cheap and safe, but homoeopaths feel that anyone wishing to experiment should learn something about the subject generally before doing so.

The appeal of homoeopathy to the agoraphobic patient lies not only in consulting someone who may be able to prescribe safe drugs to help alleviate anxiety symptoms, but also in the knowledge that the practitioner thoroughly understands the background to her condition and is able to offer sympathetic and practical advice aimed at overcoming the agoraphobia.

I am all in favour of shopping around for any kind of treatment, conventional or otherwise, which may help an agoraphobe in her search for relief from the problem. At least it shows that she is *trying* – not just sitting at home waiting for someone else to do something for her. But I would urge that you do not waste time in going from one thing to another, looking for an easy way out. Eventually you must face up to the fact that *you* have got to do most of the work yourself.

CHAPTER 9

Anything Goes

'For every ill beneath the sun
There is some remedy or none;
If there be one, resolve to find it;
If not, submit and never mind it.'
'Maxims, Morals Etc.' (1843)

James Foster, a TOD member, had an interesting story to tell about his experiences. He wrote:

While I was living in West Africa, I was still struggling with agoraphobia though disinclined to discuss it with anyone, even my own doctor who was a close personal friend.

More in the spirit of anthropological research (I told myself) than in any real hope of a cure, I decided to consult the local shaman (witch doctor).

In the rather spooky atmosphere of his home I began to wonder what I was letting myself in for, having recently seen a James Bond film in which there was a colourful but unnerving voodoo ceremony. I need not have worried; though weird there was nothing too dramatic about my treatment. I had to sit crosslegged on the floor while my 'therapist' placed a selection of dried-up herbs in my outstretched hands. I felt a bit of a ninny sitting there while he circled about me crooning and chanting under his breath. Now was the time to have a full-scale panic attack, I thought, experiencing an escalation of anxiety and looking around the claustrophobic chamber for the nearest escape route.

I stayed calm, not wanting to make an exhibition of myself – it seemed somehow ungrateful. The shaman flopped down in front of me and produced a pile of ashes out of a leather bag (ashes of what? I wondered), shuffling with them, spreading them on the floor and drawing signs amongst them with a stick.

That was the end of the first session; no noticeable improvement in my agoraphobia during the next few days and I felt a bit of a fool when I thought about it, but I went back for another session and followed up with two more. It seemed ungrateful to admit defeat, especially as he had offered to call in a second opinion, but not knowing what the 'consultant' might suggest in the way of treatment (a sacrificial cockerel and a few human bones to juggle with, perhaps) I decided to terminate the consultations and proffered my thanks to the shaman who was now richer by one watch, two shirts and a pair of shoes.

I decided to postpone any further treatment until I returned home to England.

The value of any remedy, however odd it may appear, is that the patient finds someone who will listen sympathetically and spend time discussing the problem – the time which an NHS doctor so often lacks.

Some of the therapies discussed in this chapter may seem a bit unusual, but each one of them has been tried by agoraphobes whom I have interviewed or who have written to me. At least they keep trying!

Dance therapy

When I am wound up the one way I can find relief is to switch on some music and dance around the house. Moving rhythmically eases tension and I feel quite uplifted after dancing to my favourite tunes. I particularly like Scottish country dance music even if I do finish up puffed and exhausted.

Many people go to dancing classes simply to unwind; others go for social reasons or as a means of keeping fit and lessening the physical effects of tension – especially good for agoraphobics who quite often do not take enough exercise. Dancing as a therapy in tribal communities is used to lead the participants into a trance state, the music and drumming encouraging an orgy of movement which develops into convulsions as the witch doctor and the rest of the tribe become possessed by healing spirits.

Dance therapy

In the civilized world this tradition lingered on for some time. Fits – even outbreaks of mass hysteria such as the dancing mania of the early Middle Ages – were taken to be divine visitations and had their own patron, St Vitus. But when such fits came to be regarded as a form of mental illness, dancing survived like so much else only as a ritual or pastime purged of its therapeutic content.

There have always been those who have felt that dance has a place in therapy, not just as an exercise for the body but also as an outlet for the emotions.

Bach Flower Remedies

The Remedies used are all prepared from the flowers of wild plants, bushes and trees and none of them is harmful or habit-forming.

They are used, *not directly* for physical complaints, but for the sufferer's worry, apprehension, hopelessness, irritability etc. because these states of mind or moods not only hinder recovery of health and retard convalescence, but are generally accepted as primary causes of sickness and disease.

BACH handbook

In 1930 Dr Edward Bach, a Harley Street consultant, bacteriologist and homoeopath gave up his practice and returned to his native Wales to search for flowers and trees that have healing powers. Dr Bach discovered thirty-eight herbal remedies which he developed from herbs and flowers, claiming that these could alter the disharmonies of personality and emotional states. He classified human mental conditions into seven major groups: apprehension; uncertainty and indecision; loneliness; insufficient interest in present circumstances; oversensitiveness to ideas and influence; despondency and despair; over-care for the welfare of others.

Remedies suitable for agoraphobics would appear to be:

Aspen	For apprehension and foreboding.
	Fears of *unknown* origin.
Rock Rose	Terror, extreme fear or panic.

White Chestnut	Persistent unwanted thoughts. Preoccupation with some worry or episode.
Larch	Despondency due to lack of self-confidence; expectation of failure, so fails to make the attempt . . .

At least five sufferers I know swear by the Bach remedies, claiming that they have been helped to find peace of mind; each one has been making considerable progress towards overcoming agoraphobia.

Aromatherapy

> Physicians might . . . make greater use of scents than they do, for I have often noticed that they cause changes in me, and act on my spirits . . . which makes me agree with the theory that the introduction of incense and perfume into the churches . . . was for the purpose of raising our spirits, and of exciting and purifying our senses, the better to fit us for contemplation.
>
> Montaigne, *Essay on Smells* (1580)

The essential oils or essences of plants are thought to be the very personality of the plant itself. They can be taken internally, inhaled or massaged through the skin. It has been found that much more passes through the skin than we might think possible; in France many drugs are applied to the skin surface and thus are gradually absorbed into the system. Robert Tisserand, an expert on aromatherapy, states that some oils are taken up by specific body organs, while others are distributed more generally.

After the patient's case history has been taken, the therapist selects the suitable essential oils and massages them along the spine. The oils can also be inhaled.

Maggie Tisserand in *Aromatherapy for Women* says that

essential oils are the natural alternative to tranquillizers and suggests, among others, that a few drops of geranium oil in the bath will reduce physical and mental tension and harmonize troubled emotions:

> If you have an acute attack of depression . . . then a bath in *ylang-ylang* or *clary sage* will go a long way towards making you feel better. *Jasmin oil*, although rather costly to buy, is a really excellent depression-fighter. It lifts the spirits and makes you feel really good.

According to Robert Tisserand, essential oils sprayed from an aerosol can be used in the treatment of patients suffering from anxiety or depression: 'The effect of odours on the emotions has been known for centuries, but it is only in the last thirty years or so that we have begun to realise the healing potential of this deep, inherent response to fragrance.' A TOD member comments:

> Besides my extra-strong mints which I always carry with me *à la* 'Aggie Phobie', I have a phial of basil oil to smell if I should come over faint . . . I also have a pillow filled with hop flowers to help me sleep properly. I believe this is very effective. Hop or herb pillows also make lovely presents to buy or even make yourself.

Pyramid Healing

> I spend half an hour each day sitting beneath my pyramid structure, cross-legged and with my eyes shut. I cannot tell you what this does for me in the way of relaxation. At the end of the half-hour all my tensions have gone and I feel quite euphoric.

> I know it looks weird and my family tease me, though I have caught my teenage daughter trying it out though she explained somewhat shamefacedly that it was just for a joke. No one can

deny that my agoraphobia is much improved and I go out now with scarcely any trouble; if I feel panicky feelings bubbling up I am better able to cope with them. My husband insists that it is just superstition, but I know there is more to it than that.

TOD member

Do pyramids really have some special powers? For the past fifty years men have been researching this possibility, based on the theory that certain electromagnetic waves are concentrated and condensed by the particular configuration of a pyramid. Experiments have shown that the particular shape seems to attract more of the earth's magnetic forces than we would expect, and the benefit derived from pyramids may have something to do with the balance of negative and positive ions in the air. At Leningrad University, the Russians are carrying out extensive research into pyramid energies at a large pyramid research department. A Czechoslovakian radio technician patented a cardboard pyramid-shaped razor-blade sharpener which prolongs the life of a normal blade for anything up to four months. Other experiments have shown that the taste of food can be improved if kept under a pyramidal structure and that plant growth can also be affected. It is possible to buy pyramid kits of all sizes in the form of a metal frame structure, and the literature is certainly fascinating.

Biorhythms

From the moment of birth, our 'body clocks' start to operate and our individual rhythms are established. One expert holds that 'When a person is born, the trauma of leaving the safe and warm confines of the mother's womb sets in motion a series of three cycles which will continue to recur at regular intervals until death.'

We each have a physical cycle of 23 days, an emotional cycle of 28 days and an intellectual cycle of 33 days. If charted on a graph, each circle forms a wave pattern, and it is while crossing the middle of each cycle – either from high to low or from low to high – that the individual experiences an unstable or 'critical period'; this is more significant if the 'critical' periods of two or three cycles happen to coincide on the same day. It is during these critical periods that the individual is more illness- or accident-prone, hence knowledge of one's own cycle may be useful in making decisions, for example, or in knowing when to take care to avoid stressful occasions.

Biorhythm charts are easily obtainable, and there are also small pocket calculators on which you can work out your biorhythms by keying in your birth-date and reading off your critical days.

Bouncing (Yes, bouncing!)

In a personal letter, an agoraphobic friend says:

> I have recently bought a Rebound Exerciser which is really like a mini-trampoline. I was worried about not getting any exercise as I do not get out of the house much (though I am improving). I thought the bouncer might be too energetic at first, but it is simple to control your movements and I bounce very gently, not even leaving the surface; also I hold on to the back of a chair when necessary. I feel much much fitter and it is a great way of relieving tension.

These mini-trampolines are becoming very popular for people who want to keep fit but cannot attend classes. The advertisers claim that the 'bouncers' can improve health and vitality, assist in weight loss, improve muscle tone and stimulate blood circulation *and* help to relax and relieve anxiety!

Biofeedback

Using a special electronic meter, it is possible for agoraphobics to learn to measure – and, with practice, control – their anxiety level. Anxiety causes certain changes in the body such as an increased heart rate and a galvanic skin response (GSR). You will have noticed that when you get nervous your hands become clammy; the biofeedback instrument can measure these levels of perspiration and show the amount of stress you are experiencing. There are some very simple meters which are suitable for anyone to use, while others are extremely complicated and able to monitor brainwaves.

The biofeedback instrument itself will not reduce tension or anxiety, but used in conjunction with relaxation exercises the individual can soon learn how to bring down their anxiety level.

The simplest gadget of all is a small card which it is claimed can be used to measure your state of tension. The black circle in the centre changes colour to tell you whether you are totally calm and relaxed or tense and agitated. Possibly this is a gimmick which will appeal to some agoraphobes who could carry it around and, when feeling their panic level rising, reduce it by concentrating on making the black circle change to a calming blue!

Premenstrual Tension (PMT)

Experts now believe that premenstrual tension is due to dietary deficiencies which may affect the way our hormones work and make us more sensitive to any possible fluctuations. Maryon Stewart, of the Pre-Menstrual Tension Advisory Service in Brighton, has been in contact with a number of agoraphobes who suffer from PMT and feels that there is a definite link. An independent survey of sufferers has revealed that out of 94 women, 91 per cent suffered at least one significant PMT symptom and 73 per cent said that their agoraphobia worsened during the premenstrual week.

Evening primrose oil supplements are helpful, also the B vitamins, especially vitamin B6. It is important to eat a diet which is rich in nutrients, cutting out salt, some grains, milk and sugar and concentrating on chicken, fish, brown rice and leafy green vegetables.

Maryon Stewart does not recommend vitamin supplements without studying a woman's personal profile, as vitamin imbalances vary from person to person. Details of the Pre-Menstrual Tension Advisory Service can be found in the list of useful addresses at the end of the book.

Past Lives Therapy

A TOD member relates:

If we have souls which survive death, or if reincarnation exists, it would not be surprising if traces of our past lives should periodically filter down into a present life, causing mental or emotional disturbance. Past Lives therapy is based on the assumption that some disorders arise because of past lives burrowing their way into an individual's subconscious and that these psychic intrusions may need to be brought to the surface.

I am presently working on the idea that I was a nun some five hundred years ago. You may laugh, but I am quite convinced about this. For a serious indiscretion I was banished from my convent and left to face the outside world alone. Unable to cope with this I committed suicide, but the trauma has affected all my later incarnations.

As the title of this chapter says, 'Anything Goes' and certainly agoraphobes have tried a very wide range of remedies. You may consider it flippant to include some of the above 'therapies', but the fact is that each one has been found of help to at least one agoraphobia sufferer. Their road to recovery may not be yours, but don't knock it – at least they were determined to succeed!

CHAPTER 10

Food For Thought

'I eat when I'm hungry, I drink when I'm dry,
And if the moonshine don't kill me, I'll live till I die.'
American folk song

People who are agoraphobic frequently have a weight problem. Either they are too thin because their nervous state depresses their appetite so that they eat very little – and are often heavy smokers – or at the other end of the scale they have an outsize problem with obesity. Having had many experiences of meeting agoraphobes *en masse*, these weight problems are only too evident.

Though it is fashionable to be excessively thin – to have 'a lean and hungry look' like Cassius in *Julius Caesar*, Shakespeare made Caesar say, 'Let me have men about me that are fat,' promoting the idea which has persisted through the ages that thin people are always twitchy and nervous, while the fat person has a cheerful cosy image. Both theories are untrue and both ends of the weight scale are undesirable and frequently downright dangerous.

On the whole, too much weight is the greater problem amongst the agoraphobic population. For every individual who has little appetite because of nervous tension, there are many more who eat for comfort and who – especially if they are stuck in the house all day – will make themselves endless cups of tea or coffee and nibble biscuits and sandwiches all the time as well as eating the meals they have prepared for their families. These people do of course have one particular problem which is peculiar to agoraphobes; if they have an aversion to supermarkets or shopping in a central area of the town, they are much more likely to rely on the 'little shop round the corner' where they feel safe because it is near home and there are unlikely to be crowds of other shoppers. The trouble with corner shops in town or village shops in the country is that they are limited in their stock of food-stuffs, so instead of being able to select the things needed for a well-balanced diet, our agoraphobic mother will of necessity have to feed her family on pies, sausages, fish fingers, frozen vegetables, baked beans and other convenience foods.

It is not possible to organize a healthy diet when one does not have access to fresh vegetables and meat – or, in the case of vegetarians, foods which can only be found in specialist shops. Children – and many husbands – are inclined to pick up junk food when given *carte blanche* over selecting the weekend shopping; in these cases it is imperative to plan ahead, preparing a carefully thought-out list before packing the family off to the supermarket.

Men have their own problems. Someone who is 'territorially restricted' – mildly agoraphobic, but does not like to admit it – though coping more or less normally and holding down a job, may avoid eating in public in restaurants or canteens, preferring to eat a solitary sandwich lunch or persuade colleagues to bring in takeaway meals – with chips! If he is a sociable type who can feel relaxed among friends, it is even more likely he will be found in the local pub tucking away the old favourites pies and sausages while washing them down with a couple of pints.

A problem with weight, whether too much or too little, can be devastating to an agoraphobic woman who can only too easily develop a poor self-image and let herself go –

dreading to look in a mirror and feeling progressively more depressed. Over-sensitive to the opinions of others, she is even less likely to venture outside the house in case a neighbour comments on the fact that she has lost a lot of weight, or else appears to be gaining weight. The thin woman will feel tense and miserable and go off her food for the rest of the day; the fat one will comfort herself by drinking more cups of tea and nibbling more buns and biscuits, her misery increasing along with her girth.

Having a weight problem just adds to the other worries and the agoraphobe feels even more convinced that there is no hope of her ever living a normal life. Jenny Price had reached rock bottom:

> I can hardly bear to tell fellow members of TOD that I had reached almost twenty-five stone and the fact that I had become almost completely housebound had as much to do with my appearance as the agoraphobia itself. I would only go out at the weekends when my husband would take me to have Sunday dinner with my parents. We wanted to have a baby but the problems I would have to face seemed insurmountable.
>
> My neighbour tried to persuade me to join a slimming club but I said I could not face it; apart from which I didn't know just how much I weighed (too much for my bathroom scales, I knew *that*) and what is more I didn't want to find out.
>
> Then my friend brought the local organiser of the club to see me and they bullied me gently into making the effort to go.
>
> The worst thing was finding my correct weight and I have to admit I cried all the way through that first meeting. I stayed until the end though, thanks to the sympathetic attitude of the other people there.
>
> I lost ten pounds in my first week and now eight months later I am six stones lighter. Best of all I feel so much better and am going out a little on my own. The slimming club members have been so helpful and encouraging now that they know about my agoraphobia and it would seem that every other person there has a story about an agoraphobic relative or friend.

My GP is pleased with me too and thinks we should be able to start our family before too long if I continue to make the same progress.

If you feel that you could face going to one of the excellent slimming clubs, consult any of the slimming magazines – or look in your local paper where they often advertise – to find out if there is such a club near you. There are now postal and even telephone clubs which would be even more helpful if your agoraphobia is severe; again, details and addresses of these appear in all the slimming magazines.

To suggest a specific diet which will actually help to overcome agoraphobia is unrealistic, though I know that a few years ago it was suggested on a television programme that this was possible. If you are eating or drinking anything that may affect your physical wellbeing, a sensible diet will help to put things right, but we are back to the old story – agoraphobia is a habit and it is the anxiety lying behind it which needs to be controlled. Sometimes this anxiety can be aggravated by certain substances – tea and coffee, for example, the agoraphobe's standbys!

We are warned frequently about the harm which certain foods may do if taken in excess, but beware of omitting these from your diet altogether. Extremes are always harmful, be it a case of too much or too little; vegetarians must replace meat with other protein foods, for example, while if you avoid refined sugar, this must be compensated for by taking more natural sugar in the form of fruit or honey.

In these enlightened days, and with so much advice handed out by the media about what constitutes a healthy and well-balanced diet, there is little excuse for anyone to plead ignorance of correct eating habits. However, the way in which the fashion in diets swings so violently is somewhat confusing. One year we have Dr Richard Mackarness advocating a 'stone-age' diet of meat, fat, fruit and vegetables;

now we have swung to the high fibre diet, which is precisely the opposite and has fat as enemy number one.

The current view is that a natural wholefood diet is the most beneficial – wholefoods meaning those which have had nothing added and nothing taken away. These are foods which are not processed or refined and are as near to their natural state as possible, and also foods which do not contain artificial additives such as flavourings, colourings or preservatives. Meat should be restricted to one or two meals a week, preferably poultry and lean meat only. Wholemeal bread is important as it contains natural wheat bran, the fibre which is present only in plant foods and is essential for proper digestion and elimination.

Unprocessed and unrefined natural foods contain the vitamins and minerals we use, together with fresh fruits and vegetables, beans, pulses and nuts which all contain the fibre we need.

If you are overweight, do avoid crash diets. Their success is only fleeting and you can feel nauseated and physically ill; even worse, all the agoraphobic symptoms can be accentuated in this situation. It is a wise precaution to consult your GP before embarking upon any weight-reducing programme.

Added to the overweight agoraphobe's troubles is the fact that probably she is not getting enough exercise. 'I feel so much worse if I try to exercise,' she will protest. There is a reason for this of course, because during even slight exertion the heart speeds up, she becomes warm and begins to sweat; fearing a panic attack is developing, she scares herself and starts to over-breathe which causes her to feel progressively worse. Remember that these symptoms can be controlled as we saw in Chapter 7, and remember too that gentle exercise cannot harm you; it will tone up the body and help to discharge nervous energy.

Allergies

It is now appreciated that a surprising number of people have 'hidden' allergies to a variety of different foods; some of the most common are wheat, milk, eggs, coffee, strawberries, chocolate . . . the list seems endless.

'Allergy' originally meant an unpleasant reaction to any foreign substance in the body, but doctors now use the term to describe a reaction caused by a breakdown of the immune system. A major problem arises when you become addicted to the things to which you are allergic, because these foods give you a 'high'. Unfortunately, this is only temporary and is always followed by a sharp 'low' as your body struggles to neutralize a substance which was originally a stimulant but has turned into a poison.

Many doctors still doubt the existence of such a condition as food allergy even though certain foods have been proved to have a direct link with disease. Dr Richard Mackarness's book, *Not All In The Mind*, describes how food allergy can affect both the physical and psychological state of health. His subsequent books consider the effects of other substances such as drugs, chemicals, tobacco and so on which can have a devastating effect on the human body and mind.

If you are allergic to certain foods you may well develop the same symptoms when exposed to other substances, gradually building up a whole range of different allergies; many of these can cause acute anxiety which may develop into agoraphobia.

Barbara (married and with one child) has virtually conquered her agoraphobia with little practical help from her GP. She wrote to the TOD newsletter:

I have to write and tell you of my two victories. After my last letter I was very ill again with my allergy and although my doctor admitted I did have an allergy, my unstableness (i.e.

dizziness) he said it could not possibly be caused by an allergy – it was just my nerves and I must try to battle on. He even said vitamins might help but that I must go to the chemist to buy them as I 'wasn't ill enough to have them on the NHS'. I tried everything, but I just knew this dizziness, bad eyes etc. was nothing to do with my nerves. I had learned to conquer them completely, I was sure.

I then consulted my GP's partner and again I was told the same thing 'It's your mind; all you need to be put right is ECT!' Oh dear, my husband and I had such a row with him trying to explain I had got over my agoraphobia and could now go into shops, travel and remain OK. All he said was that though I had got over that phobia another had taken its place and that I only *thought* I was dizzy.

I had found out about a special allergy unit at St Mary's Hospital, Paddington and we eventually persuaded the doctor to get me an appointment on condition that we would admit that he was right and we were wrong if the skin tests were negative.

That was December and the appointment came through for 13th May. All along I was taking anti-histamines which I persuaded the doctor to give me and was feeling really well whilst on them. He said it was the sedative effect that helped the dizziness.

. . . At the Allergy Clinic it was discovered that I have many different allergies caused not only by foods but all sorts of substances around the house. I am now receiving proper treatment and hope to feel completely normal if I take care what I eat. I have had three and a half years of unnecessary suffering but my great delight was in hearing my doctor apologise!

If you feel you may be suffering from an allergy, keep a diary listing everything you eat and drink and how you feel. By noting these details every day, you may discover if there is any link between what you eat and how you feel. If your doctor agrees that you might have an allergy, he may refer you to an allergy clinic for tests and treatment.

Hypoglycaemia

> I believe that the majority of agoraphobic sufferers are suffering
> from reactive hypoglycaemia, brought on by an excessive
> refined carbohydrate intake, or by an allergic reaction to foods
> or chemicals to which the person reacts maladaptively. Sub-
> clinical vitamin and mineral deficiency may also be present,
> particularly vitamin B-group.
> Letter from Tuula Tuormaa, Project Organizer, Coordinating
> Committee for the Advancement of Research into Agoraphobic
> Illness.

During her research Tuula Tuormaa has concluded that a
first agoraphobic attack could be caused by a sudden drop
in blood sugar (reactive hypoglycaemia), by the person
hyperventilating or more probably by a combination of
both. She suggests:

> . . . a low blood sugar (or other endocrine imbalance) could be a
> cause for the first, acute 'dizzy spells' in agoraphobia but 'the
> agoraphobic avoidance behaviour' is caused by a person hyper-
> ventilating in a situation where he feels 'trapped' and from
> where he feels he cannot escape with digniy in case another
> 'dizzy spell' might occur, i.e. out in the streets, supermarkets,
> public transport etc. Usually while preparing to go out, an
> agoraphobic has already hyperventilated to such a state of
> distress that when the time comes to leave, he is unable to do so.

Though excessive caffeine consumption and cigarette
smoking may contribute to the precipitation of acute
hypoglycaemic episodes which resemble panic attacks,
Tuula Tuormaa concludes that faulty nutrition and irregular eating habits can be said to be the single most important
cause of a low blood sugar. A glucose tolerance test is the
most reliable method for detecting this, and correct diet
will then help the patient to combat the hypoglycaemic
tendency.

Anorexia Nervosa

Several anorexic teenage girls and young women had fleeting contact with The Open Door. In most cases there were deep-seated psychological problems behind their condition and the anorexia invariably preceded their agoraphobia. Angela's letter below gives a description of how agoraphobia developed in her case; this was fairly typical of the experiences of other anorexics.

I was – am – very attached to my mother and I suppose I was spoilt as a child. I didn't like school much and was often absent with sore throats and tummy aches which meant I slipped behind more and more in my school work, except for English which was always my best subject. I love writing and enjoy getting caught up and lost in my own stories.

. . . My sister is five years younger than I am and more attractive. She has always done really well at school but I have never been jealous of her and we are very close . . . When I was about fourteen I got very fat and spotty and really hated myself. I was in trouble more and more at school because of missing so much. It wasn't that I disliked school so much – I just preferred being at home. Sometimes though on a fine day I would go for a long walk or sit in the park or public library and read.

. . . I tried different diets and started to lose weight. I hoped I would like myself more but even when I reached a normal weight I couldn't look at myself in the mirror. I wanted so much to look like my sister who was much smaller and daintier than I was.

I knew I looked awful and everyone else thought so too. My parents alternated between scolding and bribing me with promises of new clothes, money, holidays, but I didn't want to know. I stopped going out and just sat at home and read and watched television. I was six stone and the doctor said I would have to go into hospital unless I started eating. I really did try; I couldn't bear the thought of being away from home with all those people looking at me and bullying me.

Angela did go into hospital eventually, as her condition was deteriorating. She was surprised to find that she was able to cope with anxiety and panic attempts much better when away from home and this gave her the confidence to cooperate with the doctors who were treating the anorexia.

Alcohol is a Dangerous Crutch

> I keep a little hip-flask of brandy by me and when I feel jittery I have a quick swig to revive me.

> I find that a glass of sherry helps me to get through the morning but I usually need another couple of glasses at midday, another to help me get my forty winks in the early afternoon and another couple before my grown-up sons and my husband arrive home for their evening meal ... then I have to get through the rest of the evening with the family discussions, arguments and general uproar, good- or bad-tempered, all going on around me. Now by bed time I find I have finished the bottle. I seem to be on a treadmill going faster and faster and I don't know how to get off.

I find it alarming when I read of doctors who actually suggest that alcohol may be helpful in the management of agoraphobia. 'From time immemorial alcohol has been used to relieve fear and tension,' says one expert, while another writes, 'For those who are not alcoholics drink can provide a necessary safety valve from the stresses of every-day living.' Yet another admits that phobics may become addicted or alcoholic but states that if this does happen, 'They can be treated successfully by being weaned off their drugs or drink while in a sheltered environment and then have exposure treatment for their fears.'

Alcohol is a drug of dependence, which means that if a certain quantity is taken over a sufficiently long period *anyone* can become addicted. As in the case of some other drugs, this threshold can be crossed after a very short time indeed.

You may think that you feel better after a drink, but alcohol is a depressant, therefore when the initial relief of tension wears off, reaction sets in and you feel ten times worse. So what happens then? You reach for another drink; you *need* it, you *depend* on it to make life bearable. An alcoholic is someone who depends upon drink and too many women who become housebound turn to the bottle for consolation. By all means enjoy alcohol in a social situation, but never drink alone and never use drink as a crutch.

Highly strung

CHAPTER 11

Relaxation is Nature's Tranquillizer

'The cure for this ill is not to sit still,
Or frowst with a book by the fire.
But to take a large hoe and a shovel also,
And dig till you gently perspire.'

Rudyard Kipling

Kipling's advice does not seem particularly appropriate in a chapter on relaxation, but sometimes when we are all keyed up and twitchy it is necessary to work off our excess nervous energy before we can benefit from any relaxation techniques. The fact that nervous anxiety, unlike fear and normal vigilance, has no way of discharging itself means that the nervous person continually spends energy trying to control the 'fight or flight' syndrome which forms part of her anxiety. As a result, she is liable to suffer from tension states which derive as much from the need to control anxiety as they do from actually experiencing it.

'There is nothing wrong with stress and tension,' Jane Madders writes in the introduction to *Stress and Relaxation* 'They are necessary for success; but when they become excessive and prolonged or our reaction to them is inappropriate, the body protests in various ways.'

Remember how our cave man had always to be on the alert for danger? You do not have the same life-threatening situations to deal with today, but your body is reacting in the same way to the stresses and strains of your particular lifestyle and particularly to the oversensitive signals from your brain which are wrongly telling you that you are in danger.

When you learn to relax, you help your body to replace the flight response with messages to loosen tensed muscles. By releasing tension you help to signal to the mind that your situation is not dangerous, that there is no need to run away.

You may think that you are reasonably relaxed as you read this, but stop and consider what your body is doing. Your teeth are probably clenched tightly together; your tummy muscles are tensed; your shoulders hunched and knuckles white from clenched fists. Do you bite your nails, twiddle with your hair, coil your legs around each other, frown and wrinkle your forehead? Anxiety and muscle tension go hand in hand: when you are alert and on guard, the muscles tense for action and just as muscle tension is associated with arousal and anxiety, so relaxation can induce feelings of calm.

Are you sitting comfortably?

There are many books describing relaxation techniques in detail, but it is not possible to read directions and carry them out at the same time, so it is best to have a record or cassette to lead you through the exercises. The most helpful recordings are of exercises which employ progressive muscle relaxation – the systematic tensing and relaxing of each of the major muscle groups, starting at the feet and working up to the facial muscles. As you listen to the directions you will learn to tense and release each set of muscles and develop an awareness of how your muscles feel when they are taut and how they should feel when they are relaxed. As you practise, you will soon become aware of the level of tension you habitually carry within your body.

It is important to work out your own relaxation techniques and to practise the exercises that you find most comfortable. Lying on a bed or on the floor in a silent darkened room may be soothing for some people, but those who are in a nervous state may find such a setting disturbing and oppressive. Select the surroundings in which you feel most comfortable and at ease. If you find music soothing, have your favourite recording playing softly in the background until you feel ready to switch on the relaxation tape; settle yourself in a comfortable position in a chair – remember that you want to relax, not fall asleep.

Take a deep breath through your nose and release it through your mouth – allow your mouth to remain slightly open so that your jaw is not tensed up.

Do you begin to feel relaxed? No, you do not! Most phobic people become tense at the very idea of relaxing, because to them any suggestion of 'letting go' means abandoning control. Your first attempts at practising relaxation seriously may result in a heightened level of anxiety because you are not used to being without tension. You can alleviate this by demonstrating for yourself that your body, though relaxed, is still your own. Open and blink your eyes, cough or move to another position. As you do so, you will immediately find yourself back in the present and once you have satisfied yourself that you are in control, your level of anxiety will drop and you will be able to continue.

Your tape or record will concentrate firstly on relaxing your toes, then gradually work upwards instructing you to breathe evenly and calmly as you let your muscles go soft and loose – up through your whole body, arms and shoulders, neck and head. Remember that anxiety sufferers are particularly prone to tension in the head area; think of that 'tight band' around the forehead, causing those tension headaches; blurred vision; buzzing in the ears; difficulty in swallowing; a 'lump' in the throat. There is even a clinical name for the latter – *globus hystericus* – a sinister name for a lump that is not really there!

Make sure you are not gritting your teeth and let the worry muscles on your forehead relax. Now direct your thoughts to feeling the difference between tension and relaxation as you clench your teeth again and frown as hard as you can. Screw your face right up and, as you let go, really appreciate the sensation of relief.

Make your imagination work for you by picturing places and situations in which you feel happy and comfortable. It is useless trying to force yourself to relax by will-power alone; the harder you try, the more impossible it will become. Remember that your subconscious mind can only under-stand pictures, not verbal instructions, so you must feed it with scenes of tranquillity and beauty. As you are agora-phobic, you will probably be more inclined to cosy firesides than to sunlit beaches, but try gradually to be more adven-turous. When you relax, let your imagination take you to places you could not possibly go to in real life – at present; it is good practice for when you have progressed to desensi-tization in your mind.

Perhaps your imagination is a little rusty because you are not used to using it positively. You may have become so wrapped up in your fears – picturing yourself in situations which fill you with dread — that you are involved in a constant battle with your imagination, trying to keep it under control and blocking off the pictures which threaten to invade your mind. When you do reach the stage of practising systematic desensitization, whether with the help of a therapist or on your own, it is important that your imagination should be in working order.

If the picture of a sunny beach or exotic market place eludes or agitates you, go back in your memory so as to recall a time or place when you were truly happy — a particular Christmas perhaps, or some other joyful family occasion. It does not matter how far back you go so long as you can create a living memory in your mind.

Close your eyes and visualize the scene. Who else was there? What were they wearing, what would they be saying? Picture the colour of their clothes, the furniture in the room, any focal point of attention such as a Christmas tree, a table laid with food, a new baby. Can you recall the voices of the people there — what they might be saying, the sound of their laughter, the way they smiled? Try to remember a piece of music that you might associate with the occasion: there is nothing like a favourite melody to help memories to come sweeping back.

When you have tickled up your memory, when pictures in your mind become clearer and easier to conjure up, then is the time to practise projecting your imagination and visualizing events in the future instead of in the past.

Jane Madders, author of *Stress and Relaxation*, describes a technique she calls STOP! that is of special value to agoraphobics who may get 'caught short' by panic when they are in a situation from which there is no immediate escape:

STOP! AN EMERGENCY QUICK RELAXATION TECHNIQUE

There are some stressful occasions that call for a quick relaxation technique to stop a rapid build-up of tension . . . Remember that mental stress will lessen when you relax muscles. This really does happen, even when you may be in a situation where only partial relaxation is possible. Don't believe that you are the sort of person who can never relax. You can. Everyone can to some degree, but strong feelings of tension make relaxation difficult especially if they are allowed to build up. So recognise your feelings of tension (even if these seem to you to be weird and alarming). Accept them for what they are. Use the STOP! technique to lower the arousal and bring it back to manageable limits. Do this before it gets out of hand.

Say sharply to yourself, aloud if the situation permits, 'STOP!' This means stop fussing, stop getting so worked up. Then breathe in and hold your breath for a moment (generally you should *not* pause between inhaling and exhaling, but in this sort of emergency it may help. But don't hold it for more than a moment). Then breathe out *slowly* and, as you do, relax your shoulders and hands. Pause for a moment, then breathe in again. As you breathe out, slowly this time, relax your forehead and jaw. Stay quiet for a few seconds then go on with whatever you were doing, but move smoothly and slowly. If you have to talk, speak a little more slowly and with your voice a little lower than usual.

This STOP! relaxation can usually be done without anyone noticing and you will find that, in spite of your feelings the tension will lessen.

Relaxation has many benefits. Within the first week of regular practice you may discover that your general level of anxiety is lowered. After a few weeks you will be able to give yourself the mental command to relax and immediately feel the tension drain from your body. You will have fewer headaches, fewer aches and pains in your neck and shoulders, be rid of the knot of tension you once carried in your stomach – and be rid of your *globus hystericus*, that unnerving lump which is not really there!

By itself relaxation will not cure agoraphobia, but it will help you to bring down your general level of anxiety to a manageable degree.

In between your periods of relaxation practice, remember to work off some of that nervous energy we referred to at the beginning of the chapter. You may not be able to walk far because of your agoraphobia, but try to take some sort of physical exercise each day, though if you have not exerted yourself for some time be careful – do not be too energetic at first and do not frighten yourself when your body warms up and your heart beats faster than usual.

And remember – there is nothing like a good laugh to fill the lungs with oxygen and banish tension!

CHAPTER 12

Moving Towards Recovery

'A hundred-mile journey begins with one step.'
                                        Chinese proverb

If you want to get better, to live a normal life and do all the things other people do such as planning a holiday, visiting exotic countries and seeing places you have only glimpsed in books or on television, there is no reason why eventually you should not be able to do so. Some sufferers prefer to stay in the safety of their home ('she's agoraphobic, you know — poor dear!'), living a restricted life which makes few demands upon them. Living without one's problems can be hard work, because it is then necessary to find something to put in their place and this requires substantial effort.

Of course there are many people who are *not* agoraphobic who are truly content to stay put — never venturing further than a few miles from home; never in a hundred years dreaming of going abroad for a holiday. The difference is that this is the way they *want* their lives to be, so there is no reason why we should consider it in any way peculiar. *But* they are not saying, 'Agoraphobia is ruining my life and stopping me from doing the things I want to do.'

If you belong in the latter category, there is no reason why you ought to feel that foreign travel is important; it is quite possible that your partner is also uneasy at the thought of going too far from home and that is probably one of the reasons why you came together in the first place – because you were similar in temperament and had shared interests, likes and dislikes.

Whatever your eventual goal, be it Fiji or Folkestone, make your targets easy at first, but plan to tackle the important things in due course so that you would be able to cope in an emergency. Train yourself to face up to situations that are inevitably likely to crop up at some point: hospital visits, a church wedding or other family celebration, happy or upsetting occasions which are a part of life and which the average agoraphobe dreads.

Keep it simple. Don't force yourself to dream of holidays abroad; lots of people never leave this country, so don't fuss and think you are missing out – but do not fall into the trap of using agoraphobia as an excuse. You are *not* disabled. You do not need an excuse if you prefer a quiet lifestyle, and if you try to make others feel sorry for you, you will end up feeling even more sorry for yourself!

There may be reasons why you cannot cope with a recovery programme at the present time. If you have some physical condition that is aggravating your agoraphobia, or if you are trying to overcome depression, you cannot be expected to tackle the agoraphobia until the other problems – for which you should be receiving treatment – are under control. The day will come, however, when you are able to make the effort, when the will to recover will enable you to join other sufferers on the road to a normal life.

It is helpful to have someone close to offer support and encouragement, but it is by no means impossible to go it alone – indeed, some people prefer it that way. I have also known some sufferers to give up before they have even started, because unsympathetic doctors and uncaring families have made them feel that there is no one they can turn to. Our nearest may not always be our dearest, but conversely a partner who is too supportive may be just as great a hindrance to recovery:

> My husband watches me all the time when we go out and keeps asking if I feel all right, if he should go into the shops while I stay in the car. If I do feel jittery I somehow manage to communicate this to him and *he* goes pale. I find myself snapping at him, 'Oh do pull yourself together, I'm the one who's trying to fight this thing.' I know it sounds ungrateful, but frankly I'm much better practising on my own with no one to fuss over me.
>
> Sheila (35) two children.

If you love someone, it is hard to see them suffer and your family's distress at your struggles might cause them to cry, 'Stop trying, it is not worth the effort. We are happy as we are.' Children who are used to their mother being permanently at home may feel insecure if she starts to behave out of character and leaves the house to go shopping or visit friends. A husband may subconsciously prefer to have a wife who is totally dependent upon him; if she kicks the agoraphobia habit, he could see this as a threat to his settled way of life:

> George really likes me to be at home all the time. His mother never had a job and was always pottering about the house sewing and cooking – as far as I could see quite contented with her lot. She and his father went away for two weeks every summer; always to the same place and that was the extent of their outings. George cannot understand why I fret so; there are so many things I'd love to do, but I feel he is deliberately holding me back.
>
> Gladys (38), no children.

> When I grow up I'm going to get married and have six children and stay at home and never have to go out like Mummy.
>
> Claire (6).

Mothers of young children represent the strongest and the weakest members of the agoraphobic population. At one end of the scale, there is the woman who is making tremendous efforts to recover in order that her family may have a normal background with a mother who can be relied upon to take them out, organize their school and social lives, always be relied upon in an emergency. At the other end is the mother who finds it quite impossible to cope on her own; in fact she never goes out – neither do her children when they are very young – and when they are old enough to go to school she cannot bear to be separated from them and often keeps one (usually the eldest girl) at home with her for company, thus running into all sorts of trouble with the school authorities. Her reason is that she cannot be left on her own, that she must have her daughter with her, and she is unable to see the damage she is doing to the child quite apart from the obstacles she is putting in the way of her own recovery.

Agoraphobia is not an hereditary illness, but we can pass on a nervous and highly-strung disposition to our children. If we let them see that we are disturbed, they will pattern their behaviour on ours and will inevitably display agoraphobic tendencies later in life when they are under stress.

One of the reasons why it is so difficult to treat agoraphobia is that sufferers react in totally different ways, and their view of their predicament may be quite different from that of another person with a similar background and the same symptoms.

The following letters are from TOD members both in their mid-thirties and each with two children:

I feel like a prisoner in my own home. My husband has to get on with his life outside, our children have to manage without me to take them to school or parties, and we have to make special arrangements when they need to see a doctor or go to the dentist. They have to help their father with the shopping and I feel so helpless and useless. I live in terror that one day I am going to have to face an emergency in the family. My mother lives nearby and she does a lot for me, but she is getting on and what am I going to do if she falls ill or gets too old to be my support? Sometimes I feel suicidal.

Some women make a dreadful fuss about agoraphobia. I say they should just accept it and make the best of life. I am totally housebound, but I have a loving husband and two teenage sons who are very good. They know Mum is always around if they need me and although I know they have to do things other boys don't, especially at the weekends when I need them to run errands and help their Dad with the shopping, it is good training for them later on if they ever have families of their own.

The boys go on school trips and go away for sports holidays. Luckily my husband isn't keen on holidays, as he enjoys doing things around the house and working in the garden. I run a mail order catalogue, so all my shopping needs are catered for. I am really quite content.

Which of these two women do you feel sorry for? In fact it was the first one who – without any treatment apart from support from her GP – got herself going with the help of Dr Claire Weekes' books and cassettes. She later wrote:

I know I still have a long way to go but I have made so much progress and have a real sense of achievement knowing that I have done it all on my own. I take Dr Weekes' advice and float through the odd panic which still knocks me about once a week. The important thing is that I am not afraid of the panics any more – understanding the fear of fear and knowing how to cope with it makes all the difference. Also, instead of fretting about what might have been and what might be in store in the future, I take one day at a time, looking forwards to the day when I know I shall be free of this wretched complaint.

If you are feeling that life is passing you by and that you are getting no better, that there is no prospect of treatment and little in the way of outside support, be comforted by what Professor Eysenck has to say in *You and Neurosis*:

> The first and most important fact about neuroses is that they are self-limiting; in other words, sufferers tend to get better without any form of psychiatric or medical treatment . . . on the whole some two out of three neurotics, suffering from fairly serious to very serious disorders, improve greatly or recover completely over a period of two years or so.

We did find in TOD that two years was a fair average from the onset to the relief of most symptoms in 20 per cent of all members. For those who had become totally housebound, thirteen years was nearer the mark.

It is unfortunate that any survey conducted amongst agoraphobes is concentrated on the acute and long-term sufferers who either are receiving treatment or are members of one of the phobic organizations. Those people who have been affected by agoraphobia, struggled with it and recovered within a two-year period are rarely involved in such surveys, so the resulting statistics seem particularly gloomy. It may be argued that because their lives are not noticeably disrupted these short-term sufferers cannot be classed as true agoraphobes, but I can assure you that being able to hide your symptoms and keep going does not mean that you are not involved in a distressing and uphill struggle to preserve a normal lifestyle.

I consider it pointless to quote results from past surveys, because I do not believe that these have any significance. If a national publication – one of the Sunday newspaper magazines, perhaps – was to conduct a survey asking for co-operation from anyone female *and* male who has experienced agoraphobic symptoms, however mild, I believe we would begin to get a true and much more encouraging picture of the incidence of complete recovery.

There are a few cases of spontaneous recovery amongst past TOD members. This usually happens as a result of severe shock – usually an unpleasant one. The death or departure of a partner who has provided comfort and support for years might be expected to have a disastrous effect upon the agoraphobe, but occasionally it has resulted in the person being catapulted into the outside world where she has been forced to start a new life. In some cases the phobia has faded completely; one TOD area secretary wrote to me:

> Do you remember how worried we were about Jean six months ago when her husband was killed in an accident involving his lorry? We all thought Jean would go under – she had been virtually housebound for two years and depended on her husband for everything.
> . . . Well, you will be pleased to know that Jean is now working! She just erupted out of her house one day and found herself a job. Ray's death was the worst thing that had ever happened to her, she says, and the agoraphobia lost its hold after that . . .

There was also the particularly sad case of a widow whose teenage son killed himself while experimenting with explosives at the bottom of the garden. Until then she had spent her life worrying about him; when he died there was nothing left to worry about . . . and her agoraphobia disappeared.

Another mother wrote:

> The school nurse telephoned to say Jason had walked into a glass door and was bleeding badly. The ambulance was on its way and would I go to the school at once, so I could accompany

him to the hospital. I did not feel what I always thought of as panic; just a sort of white-hot hammer banging my whole system.

My next-door neighbour took me to the school in her car and all I could think of was what if an artery had been severed. I can honestly say that I never even considered my agoraphobia. Luckily things weren't as bad as feared and I spent the rest of the day with Jason at the hospital while he was stitched up and we both recovered from the shock.

When Mike got in from work he said he was proud of us both for being so brave. 'I always knew you were as tough as old boots,' he told me. My self-esteem has soared and I feel ready to do battle with my old enemy.

There is no denying that for most of us it is important to have someone to turn to for reassurance and encouragement. Anyone involved in one of the self-help organizations for phobia sufferers will tell you that the first reaction of new members is to say, 'Thank God someone knows how I feel . . .' It is such a relief to write it all down, talk to another sufferer, read about the ways in which other phobic people cope. Often such people have suffered alone for years, not realizing how many other people shared the same symptoms and not knowing that anything could be done to help them.

If you intend to make contact with one of these organizations, find out if it has the backing of doctors or psychiatrists. If there are therapeutic groups, check that they are supervised by someone who is qualified – there are too many amateur psychologists around who think that they can help, but this can be dangerous when such people start delving into background anxieties without knowing how to help the patient resolve any problem that may be unearthed.

If you are particularly impressionable and over-sensitive, do not be persuaded into making contact with other sufferers who may want to discuss symptoms interminably, give adverse reports on treatments that they or others have tried and failed, and discourage you from embarking on similar treatment which might be suitable in your case. Especially you need to avoid those people who have been agoraphobic for more than five or six years and who have made little or no progress towards recovery. I was once accused on a television programme of starting a cult, and unfortunately there is no doubt that some people who have accepted agoraphobia as a way of life are inclined to encourage others to do the same.

None of the self-help organizations want to be used as an emotional dustbin, but they all collect their quota of problem members who can quickly spread alarm and despondency throughout the rest. If you feel that you would like to help others who are in a worse position than yourself, that is great; but if your own progress is being hindered by others who are endlessly drawing on your time and sympathy, back out quickly.

On the positive side, these organizations can offer information and advice, details of treatment and addresses of hospitals where it is available. Some have the backing of doctors and professional assistance in planning self-help programmes.

If you wish to make contact with a specific organization, I would suggest that you write to the problem page of one of the women's magazines or the national press to find out if it is still in operation – they do come and go – and obtain the current address.

Feelings of Unreality

Depersonalization – the medical term for unreality – is frequently mentioned in books on agoraphobia, but it is rarely described satisfactorily and someone experiencing this for the first time is usually convinced that she is going mad. The fact that no one understands when she tries to explain the sensation, makes her feel even more isolated and peculiar. As mentioned earlier, I personally liken the feeling to that of 'going under' an anaesthetic, a heavy nightmare sensation where everything around you is out of focus, you cannot feel the ground under your feet and nothing seems real – especially you. It is one of the most unpleasant sensations, feared and dreaded by most agoraphobes, and one of the most disturbing features is that it can strike without warning and without any undue build-up of anxiety or feelings of panic.

The sensation can last for an hour or just a few seconds – a sudden flash of disorientation which passes so quickly that there is no time to experience any accompanying panic, merely a kind of shocked surprise. At other times the sufferer can remain in a state of unreality for several hours or even several days, usually when the attack has been preceded by a period of acute anxiety and tension, some-times by a debilitating physical illness. The nervous system becomes so over-sensitized that the slightest thing can trig-ger off blasts of unreality. A sudden noise, a light being switched on, someone coming into the room suddenly – all these can provoke a reaction which results in the sufferer feeling totally disorientated. The sensation can strike even when you are just dropping off to sleep, jerking you into a waking nightmare where you do not know where you are and your heart is thudding uncontrollably. Sometimes your memory can black out for a few seconds – I wrote earlier of having to carry a card around with me at one time so as to keep me in touch with reality – but everything always returns to normal after a few minutes and once you have learned to face these sensations and not try to fight or run away from them, you will gradually lose your fear and learn to accept them calmly.

Remember the mythical agoraphobe 'Aggie Phobie'? Her

collection of props which had always to accompany her were her protection against 'unreality'. A shopping trolley or push-chair gives her something on which to grip and steady herself; an umbrella provides a roof when the sky seems too large and overpowering; sunglasses are also an added protection. The lady usually carries a newspaper or magazine to take her mind off herself and reassure her that the rest of the world is operating normally. If she is not worried that other people might consider her eccentric, she may wear mini-earphones connected to a transistor radio. Smelling salts and extra-strong peppermints are probably a 'must' in her handbag, providing a quick jolt back to reality when necessary.

Pets can be Agoraphobic too

Many agoraphobic sufferers own a dog, relying on their pet for companionship on therapeutic walks. I must offer a word of warning here: dogs are very sensitive creatures and apt to pick up their owner's vibrations. I had a miniature poodle to help me keep going at one time, taking her out every evening as I worked on extending my limits. Although I travelled into London to my job each day, during bad patches I found it difficult to walk any distance locally. Within a few months the dog had become even more neurotic than I was and it was she who eventually became housebound while I had to press on with my walks alone.

When I mentioned my agoraphobic poodle to my phobic friends, I discovered several cases of similarly afflicted pets; there seemed an obvious answer – pick one of the 'tough' breeds instead of the more nervous types. Or is this too simple? Liz, an 'ex-Aggie', tells:

Agoraphobic dog

I have a white bull terrier – 'Butch'. He is very fierce with strangers and with other dogs, but he has a problem . . . he will only walk in the park. I have to wheel him along the road to the park in a baby buggy and once inside the gates he will romp quite happily in his 'non-phobic' area, getting into the buggy when it is time to return home.

Holidays

Holidays? Out of the question, you might think, but it is surprising how many people with quite severe agoraphobia manage to travel long distances to spend a holiday away from home. If their background anxiety has worn off to some extent, they can escape from their phobic situations for a while. In different surroundings there has been no time to build up new spots to avoid, no time to develop the phobic habit.

'I can't even shop by myself at home, but look where I am now!' announced one postcard from Morocco. 'I've even ridden on a camel!'

Anticipation is quite the worst part of planning a holiday. The average sufferer will spend many a sleepless night, dream up every excuse in the book for cancelling the expedition. What a shame it is when you realize that to everyone else the planning is one of the most exciting and enjoyable parts of going away . . . However, if our agoraphobe does reach the fatal day without opting out, if she does make a supreme effort, she may surprise even herself. The journey may be misery, but once she has reached her destination and settled in she could actually discover that she is having fun.

A self-catering holiday will obviously have the greatest appeal, whether it is spent on a narrow boat moving slowly through the peaceful countryside or in a holiday camp chalet – surprisingly perhaps, some agoraphobics *do* enjoy a holiday camp atmosphere! Penny, aged 20, is an example:

> There I was up on the platform with all those people looking at me. 'Miss Roly Poly Ponting'. What a title to win! 'Better than Miss Aggie Phobie,' said Dave. He is so proud of me for entering the contest . . . we have been through so much together fighting my agoraphobia.

My first holiday away from my family was in Wales with my then fiancé and his parents. At twenty-three, I had never been away from home on my own! They had no idea that I had agoraphobia; even Michael had not guessed there was anything wrong and I would have died rather than admit to it. What did Michael want to do? Walk up Snowdon! Not even to go up by the little train, but to walk up the mountain path – five miles up and five miles down. And I could not walk across Parliament Square to the Foreign Office where I worked without experiencing the whole range of panic, jelly-legs, dizziness *et al*, every single morning of the week!

I made it to the top and back – cool, calm(ish) and cheerful. As long as I kept my eyes down, I did not get the feeling that I was about to fall off the side of the mountain and I even ate my sandwiches while perched on the summit.

I have to admit that I could not get down the track fast enough, despite my blistered feet and Michael's protests that I was being much too energetic. What an achievement! The following week I was tottering past Big Ben in my usual state of jitters.

One TOD member recounts how she travelled on a plane

A seat by the door

for the first time. Though she considered herself a recovered agoraphobe, she requested a seat by the door when she boarded the plane – to the consternation of the stewardess and the amusement of her husband who never let her forget the episode.

Perhaps you feel that you could never contemplate leaving the safety of your home to go on holiday? We all change if given the chance; sometimes we can hardly recognize the person we were just a few years ago.

Remember the schoolgirl who panicked when she saw an accident? That was me. For years afterwards I really dreaded having to pass the scene of an accident; I would go out of my way in case I saw something nasty. Then one day I was waiting to cross a road when a motorcyclist rode straight under a bus and I ran . . . towards him!

CHAPTER 13

Get Up and Go!

*'To rely totally upon a professional for help is to declare
one's dependence upon that person; to acknowledge that
self-help is possible is to acknowledge that one is not
totally powerless but can and must make a substantial
contribution to the effort to escape from the disorder
and its disabling effects.'*

Dr Ross Mitchell, *Phobias*

Now is the time to put into practice all the things you have
been promising yourself you will try to do – *when* you are
ready. You will never be ready while you just sit around
waiting for the right moment; the probability is that you just
do not know where to begin; so let us tackle some of the
basic steps one at a time.

Face up to Your Fears

Fear of fear itself is the most disabling problem of all and is
really tied up with a dread of the unknown. Perhaps you
have even reached the state where a knock on the front door
or the ring of the telephone sends the familiar flash of fear
zipping through you; your mind seizes up, your heart thuds,
your mouth goes dry. Who is at the door? What do they
want? I can't face them! This is an extreme reaction, of

course, but many of us can recognize similar responses in a milder form.

However unpleasant an impending event threatens to be, when you actually face it you find it is never so bad as you expected. Most phobic people experience their worst fears when imagining how they *might* feel when confronting their dreaded object or situation. There are times when even a non-phobic person will say, 'The suspense is killing me!' Of course they do not mean it literally, but the agoraphobe feels that this statement may not be far from the truth. The anticipation is far worse than the actual happening.

You may be one of those people who are nervous and avoid reading anything about agoraphobia in case they upset themselves by discovering some terrible fact such as: *Agoraphobia is a killer disease!* or *Every agoraphobe faces the probability of being housebound for life.* It isn't! They don't! You must learn to accept the true facts – that most agoraphobia sufferers are normal people with an over-sensitized nervous system and an out-of-control imagination.

You may well read about unpleasant symptoms from which others suffer, and which you have not experienced; there is no need to add them to your own collection. The more you learn about agoraphobia, the less of a shadowy and threatening demon it will become.

Stop feeling sorry for Yourself

'I cried because I had no shoes, until I met a man who had no feet.' This is another Chinese proverb that says it all. You are not disabled; you are not an invalid. Too many agoraphobes demand sympathy and put up a constant cry, 'When are "they" going to do something to help us?' Of course you need help – positive help in the way of treatment, support and encouragement – but I am afraid I do not go along with the idea that agoraphobes should be considered permanently disabled. How could you want to be so labelled?

Develop compassion for those suffering from illnesses which do mean that they will never be able to live a normal life – *you* can recover! Do not listen to the miseries who tell you that agoraphobia will be a part of your life for evermore; recovery is possible, even if it does take time. Remember that if you are housebound and suffering from disabling anxiety that prevents you from living a normal life, this is a pathological anxiety state and needs treatment.

One of the reasons why general practitioners appear unsympathetic is that they do hate their patients to give themselves labels; many doctors really dislike the term agoraphobia because they know that what they are being asked to treat initially is the phobic habit rather than the anxiety state. Medication where necessary, explanation and reassurance will help to prepare the patient for the next step towards tackling agoraphobia; a good GP will then find out where specialist treatment is available.

Consider your Family

Does your partner really enjoy doing the shopping by himself? Do you burden him with the task of making excuses for you whenever there is a crisis to cope with, people to face, a school open day or an office party?

John is a tower of strength. I never have to feel guilty about my restricted lifestyle, as he is prepared to take over all the chores I would otherwise have to cope with. He stands up for me when nosey relatives who don't understand agoraphobia are critical, and he explains why I am not like other people as I have this dreadful handicap . . .

TOD member who shall remain nameless

If your husband is like John, he needs therapy just as much as you do!

Stop trying to convince yourself that your children prefer to have a mother who can be guaranteed to be always at home; that the family really do not want to go away for a holiday. They may all rush to your defence because 'poor mother' must not be upset as her nerves are bad, but take a good look at the ways in which their lives are being restricted because of you.

With the best intentions the family could be holding you back, preventing your recovery by convincing you that you are too sick to make the effort. Again we have Elizabeth Barrett as an example; she was rapidly going downhill, a permanent invalid coddled by her oppressive father and encouraged by her brothers and sisters to consider herself a dying cripple. However, as soon as Robert Browning entered her life, she realized that she could get better.

Perhaps your family is thoroughly unpleasant. They may be horrid to you, unwilling to understand your problems, actively unsympathetic and unsupportive. Or you may be all alone with nobody to care about you. What a good excuse to wallow in self-pity! *You* have even more reason to make an effort to recover.

Harness your Imagination

'Cowards die many times before their deaths,' wrote Shakespeare. A vivid imagination can be a curse; it is up to you to change its direction and learn to control it so that it becomes a source of pleasure and inspiration.

Your subconscious mind is incapable of distinguishing between a real or an imagined experience; everything your conscious mind tells you, your subconscious will believe and accept as fact. If you imagine you are ill, you will feel ill; if you picture the places where your agoraphobia strikes, your subconscious mind will believe you and the message will go out to your body to react. Now here come the jelly-legs, the overbreathing, the dizziness. You cannot control your subconscious mind by will-power; giving it instructions will not work, as it does not understand words, only pictures. Many people assume that will-power should help them to overcome their problems; when it does not, they blame themselves for lacking strength of character . . . they are trying to open a door with the wrong key.

If you do not believe me, try a small experiment. See if you can make your mouth water by using will-power. Think about it hard, instruct it to water; keep telling yourself that you are determined, that the saliva is flowing and your will-power is winning . . . but it isn't!

Now imagine your favourite food; create a picture in your mind and concentrate on it. Look at the pattern on the plate, visualize the food – how tempting it looks, how delicious it smells! See yourself sitting down at the table preparing to enjoy your meal; you may think of roast beef and Yorkshire pudding, fish and chips or pickled herrings – or even a nut cutlet. As you imagine the flavour when you take that first mouthful, you will find that your mouth starts to water.

Here is another experiment to prove to yourself the power of your imagination. Close your eyes and walk in a straight line, pretending that you are strolling down a garden path or walking across a large room. Quite simple, you say. Now do the same thing again, imagining that you are on a tight-rope fifty feet above the ground, with traffic moving below you and people pointing upwards as you take your first tentative step. How far can you get?

When you have a few quiet minutes to yourself, practise using your imagination to visualize the situations in which you feel happy and at ease; sink into a daydream and see yourself relaxed and happy, doing the things you most enjoy.

Keep a Diary

I do not mean here a printed diary with a couple of lines for each day, but a large exercise book in which you can let yourself go when writing about your daily life. Nothing to write about? Once you get going, you will be surprised just how much there is. 'Today is the first day of the rest of my life' may sound corny, but write this at the top of the first page and look on your diary as a chart of your recovery.

Those of us who have been avid diarists since childhood may look back at our adolescent recordings and laugh at entries such as, 'Horrible day, beastly school, I hate so-and-so'. Life's unpleasant aspects were all faithfully logged, but as we matured our outlook changed if we were lucky and we became more positive.

When I was a dreary, neurotic seventeen-year-old, I decided to try to find just one thing which pleased me each day, and to write about this in my diary which was becoming a repository of gloomy observations and dire predictions about my future. The positive list began to grow as I developed the habit of recording pleasant happenings and more cheerful thoughts. It need only have been a piece of music which I found uplifting, buying some flowers, receiving a compliment or reading something interesting or entertaining in a newspaper or magazine. Gradually I stopped moaning on paper.

It is not easy to practise positive thinking when you have been so wrapped up in your fears that you have felt too exhausted to think constructively at all – so start small, at first finding as I did just one item to look back on which had brightened the day.

Chart your Progress

Use your diary to plan your recovery. Do not look too far ahead or you will be discouraged. There is no point in imagining yourself viewing the Taj Mahal by moonlight; it would have no appeal to you at present, because you would only start to panic thinking how ill you might feel so far from home!

The specialists say that you should make a list of things you cannot do and situations you cannot face; put them in order of difficulty and, starting with the least upsetting one, gradually work your way through it. However, this is not always the best approach, because the typical agoraphobe, instead of concentrating on the first item on her list, will start to worry about the rest. It is one thing to walk alone to the corner shop and then back home; but when you know that as you progress down the list you will be expected to get on a bus and spend the whole day shopping in town, your mind will be thinking ahead and telling you that there is no way will you ever be able to face such an ordeal.

So, take one step at a time; what will you tackle first? It might be walking a mile on the common; it might be staying in the house completely on your own for a whole day. Decide on your first venture, plan exactly what you are going to do and make up your mind to start . . . tomorrow? Not likely; once you have decided to get going, do it straight away! There is no point in back-pedalling and making up excuses to put things off; do you really think you will be successful if you have had a sleepless night rehearsing in your mind the ordeal you have planned for the morning?

Ready to do Battle?

Forget it! It is no good attacking agoraphobia with a grim determination to overcome it at all costs: it will just fight back and you will be beaten before you start. If you prepare to fight, your body will tense up and the physical symptoms will also prepare for action and swamp you. Gritting your teeth will only give you a pain in the neck, so relax, breathe deeply and keep calm. *Now* you are ready to go.

Get Set to Go

Have you finally decided on your first goal? The letter box around the corner, perhaps, or some place you have not walked to unaccompanied for ages. At first you will be tempted to tackle the exercise in a rush, overbreathing like mad as you scuttle round the corner, touch the letter box and rush back home as fast as you can. No panic? Great! But why do you feel so grotty? The panic did not materialize, but the anticipation of how you *might* have felt was almost as bad as the real thing.

Before you try again, sit down and go through your relaxation exercises. When you feel rested, calm and comfortable, picture yourself walking over the route you have just covered; see yourself tranquil and confident, breathing normally and walking briskly without hurrying. When you reach the letter box, stand there for a few minutes; do not flee for home straight away, but look around and make a mental picture of the houses and gardens, fixing in your mind the colour of the front door or the nearest house, which flowers are blooming in the garden, what make of car is standing outside. Concentrating on a specific task will take your mind off any lurking symptoms which might be waiting to materialize. Still in your imagination now, turn back and walk home feeling really pleased with yourself.

Desensitization in fantasy

As you reward yourself for the success of your mental trip with a cup of tea, think how much easier the walk will be when you do it properly tomorrow. Tomorrow? There you go again; you are going to do it today – right now! Who said it was against the rules to do the exercise more than once a day? Off you go again – not in your comfortable chair, but on your own two feet. Don't forget to stop when you get there; what was the colour of that front door?

'I walked to the letter box around the corner today,' you

will write in your diary. 'Twice! The front door of the house nearby was red, the car was a Ford and there were no flowers in the garden, just a droopy shrub in the middle of a tired patch of grass.'

As you repeat the exercise on following days, make a note of things to look out for: dogs, children on bicycles, delivery vans and so on. Note them all in your diary when you return home. When you are ready to proceed to the next step, it must of course be more difficult than the first, but with any luck you will have built up just a little more confidence and determination to go further and stay out longer.

Again practise your imaginary trip when you are in a relaxed state, but this time visualize how you would react if the dreaded panic struck. See yourself waiting calmly for the anxiety to subside, breathing regularly and not panicking. On no account try to run away from the feelings because they will only stay with you and follow you all the way home, causing you to feel ten times worse, so it is vitally important that you learn to feel relaxed and confident before tackling real situations.

It is only to be expected that at first you will make many swift escapes when you feel anxiety building up, and it is inevitable that there will be times when you experience bad panic attacks. When this happens it is important that you do not feel that you have failed and that your efforts at helping yourself are pointless. There *will* be setbacks, and you must learn to accept them as a necessary part of recovery. Learning to cope with unpleasant feelings will ensure that you are prepared if they strike again at some time in the future.

Perhaps you will never again experience panic; agoraphobia has been known to burn itself out without the sufferer even realizing that she is better, so long as she remains restricted to her 'safe' situations, unwilling to test her reactions further afield and not appreciating that she is now free. Habit and the fear of fear have been her jailers.

However, most of us have to shed our fears gradually, pushing ourselves just a bit further each day until we can face unpleasant symptoms with no more than a feeling of irritation, refusing to be panicked into trying to escape and knowing that if we stand up to our fears they will quickly subside.

Some sufferers will have the benefit of qualified therapists to help them plan their recovery and be on hand to provide support and encouragement; others may rely on a sympathetic partner, families or friends to pick them up, dust them down and cheer them on when necessary and provide a shoulder to cry on when the way ahead seems too difficult to tackle.

But if you have to go it alone, do not be deterred from

Today is the tomorrow you worried about yesterday

trying. There are many agoraphobes who are able to call on professional and family assistance, but who prefer to work through their recovery without involving anyone else. *It can be done.*

The world is full of recovered agoraphobes, myself included, who can look back and feel that the phobic period in our lives, though unpleasant, represented a challenge which we accepted, and that having overcome our fears we found ourselves stronger. Everyday anxieties which we all have to face from time to time can never be as bad as the old terrifying irrational fears and panics which once seemed to dominate our lives. We cope with them, put them aside and get on with living without worrying about disasters and problems that *might* lie ahead. Enjoy your freedom!

Conclusion

In this book we have been looking at the *habit* of agoraphobia though there are of course, many people who are suffering from physical and psychological disorders which must be treated before the agoraphobia itself can be tackled. Let us have a résumé of the agoraphobia syndrome:

1 The anxiety.
2 The panic with all the accompanying symptoms and overwhelming sense of disaster.
3 Because the subject feels intense fear which she associates with the location where the original panic occurred, this place acts as a trigger to panic attacks on future occasions.
4 She avoids the scene of the original panic.
5 The panic recurs in another place – hence another place to be avoided.
6 The habit of agoraphobia is built up.

The message is that you *can* recover from agoraphobia and lead a normal life. There is a way if you are prepared to make the effort to find it – as long as you do not rely on other people to produce a formula for instant recovery.

Agoraphobia itself is not a disabling disease: those who become housebound are invariably suffering from a chronic anxiety state and these people should not be confused with others who are in a position to cope with a reasonable level of anxiety and tackle their phobia. Do not expect results too quickly; you must realize that you cannot eliminate anxiety completely, but that you have to learn to live with it and accept it until gradually you get it under control.

Although there is still an urgent need for improved facilities for the treatment and support of agoraphobia sufferers, it is vitally important that the condition should be recognized in the early stages before it is allowed to get a firm hold. We have seen how anxiety in children can develop into school phobia and progress to agoraphobia; how shock or illness can result in sudden panic attacks. Early recognition and treatment of an anxiety state and sympathetic handling in the early stages of agoraphobia could help many to avoid joining the ranks of the housebound.

I have made a cassette recording which I hope some of you might find helpful. Also called 'Who's Afraid of Agoraphobia' it follows on from this book to help you plan a recovery programme and provide the encouragement to help you on your way. Details are obtainable from the address below:

4 Manorbrook,
Blackheath
London SE3 9AW   Alice Neville

What the Experts Say

What may have caused the first panic? General anxiety; a traumatic experience, accident or operation; emotional problems; illness; prolonged period of stress, say the sufferers themselves. What do the experts say?

. . . In the vast majority of my agoraphobic patients the cause was neither deep-seated nor difficult to find. Their agoraphobia was the result of severe sensitisation suddenly or gradually acquired and kept alive by bewilderment and fear.
Claire Weekes, *Agoraphobia, Simple and Effective Treatment*.

Your panic can be understood only when it is seen in its right context – that is, in the light of an earlier emotional experience which was so devastating that it was heavily repressed. It has been 'forcefully forgotten' by the conscious mind, but the memory of it is stored away in the unconscious; it still forms part of your experience . . . Your *intense panic* will only make sense when the real meaning of it is discovered.

Muriel Frampton (psychologist),
Agoraphobia; Coping with the world outside.

The anxieties can be cleared by working on the assumption that the sufferer needs to get used to the situation which troubles him, without any need to reconstruct his personality.

Isaac Marks, *Living With Fear*

(Results of research) indicate that the very first 'agoraphobic attacks' could be caused by (i) sudden drop in blood sugar (Reactive hypoglycaemia),

(ii) a person hyperventilating

or, which is more likely, a combination of both.

Tuula Tuormaa, *Journal of Alternative Medicine*
January 1984.

The claim made by Blythe & McGlown (1982), that there is an organic basis – dysfunction of the central nervous system with accompanying balance and motor system disturbances and oculo-motor problems – underlying the presenting symptoms in certain cases of agoraphobia, is undoubtedly a controversial one. It is, to a degree, running against the currently accepted theories of the origins and nature of agoraphobia. However, it is a neurologically accepted fact, that the continued presence of primitive reflexes in older children and adults is indicative of either a pathology or marked central nervous system dysfunction, and that patients, who have been diagnosed as suffering from a variety of psychopathological disorders, have been subsequently found to have detectable CNS dysfunctions.

Marie Ljunggren (Swedish psychologist)
(The above is an extract from her M.Sc. thesis)

Sufferers will no doubt pick the theory which most appeals to them and where possible choose the therapy they feel will be of most help in their particular case.

Recovery

It is difficult to say how many agoraphobics make a complete recovery; how many can look back on the phobic period of their lives and be able to say 'I am completely free of it.'

Statistics are based of course on the case histories of the agoraphobes who receive treatment, and do not take into account the hundreds – thousands – who suffer from mild agoraphobia for a few months, a couple of years and who never tell anyone about it; they just hope that it will wear off and are relieved when it does.

I am afraid that there are some agoraphobes who will not recover completely because they are not prepared to make more of an effort. Their motto might well be, 'If I don't try I cannot be said to have failed.' Joy Melville in her book *Phobias* says:

> One theory about agoraphobia is that it can be a subconscious safeguard *against* a fear, or failure – a way of avoiding carrying out certain duties or tasks and a protection against these . . . Agoraphobia can also be used subconsciously, as a reason for not taking that better job, or indeed, *any* job; or not having to leave the security of the home and go out, especially in a strange district; or not having to socialise.

Ruth Hurst Vose has a similar view:

> Agoraphobia can be a convenient, if drastic excuse not to take on a new job or responsibilities. It also can be used as blackmail to ensure the devotion of people around you. Agoraphobia makes sure you are the centre of attention in the family whether you like it or not, and some emotionally inadequate people would find they had no limelight in life at all without it.

This is sad but true; I have met many agoraphobes who were just like this. They grab the handle of agoraphobia and convince themselves and everyone around that they are severely disabled and that life should revolve around them. It is such a pity that when the majority are struggling to get back to normal living, a few should present a picture of the 'typical agoraphobe' as someone who has thrown in the sponge – who is making no effort to recover.

Recovery is hard work and often disappointing because of the fluctuating character of agoraphobia. One day you feel you can face the world and tackle anything, another all you want to do is hide away. Unfortunately there is no easy way out.

'Modern psychiatry is leaning more and more to the idea that people should be able to take control of their lives without spending hours of agonised delving into their pasts,' writes Dr Garth Wood, author of *The Myth of Neurosis, a Moral Therapy*. He continues:

> Surely we must come to terms with the fact that life was not designed to be easy or even pleasant, and that happiness and contentedness must be earned. How different is the generally accepted theory that we have a natural right to a life free of psychological pain, a view that leads us to consult the 'experts' whenever we experience it.
>
> ... In most cases, therefore, we should not be afraid of anxiety, nor should we consider it abnormal, nor without use. Instead we should regard it as a spur to action, an unpleasant experience whose job it is to get us moving. Our anxiety should lead us to a brave confrontation of our problems and increase in our self-respect. Having performed its function, it will then disappear with the net result that we like ourselves more.
>
> Always we must avoid the mistake of concentrating on the anxiety itself and turning *that* into our problem. Encouraged by the constant expressions of the introverted psychobabble of the mind pundits, many of us end up worrying more about our anxiety than about getting on with our lives and behaving as we believe we should. 'I can't do anything to get rid of my anxiety because I am so incapacitated by it' is often the attitude.

Dr Wood emphasizes that this does not apply to patients suffering from a genuine pathological anxiety state but as we know, in many cases of agoraphobia the anxiety state has faded . . . we are left with the habit, the habit that must be conquered.

Books to Read

Agoraphobia, Vose, Ruth Hurst
(Faber & Faber Ltd, 1981)

Acupuncture, Cure of Many Diseases, Mann, Felix
(Pan Books Ltd, 1978)

Agoraphobia – An Organic Basis?, Ljunggren, Marie
(Psychological Institute, Gothenberg University, 1982)

Agoraphobia: Coping with the World Outside, Frampton
Muriel
(Turnstone Press Ltd, 1984)

Agoraphobia: Simple, Effective Treatment, Weekes, Claire
(Angus & Robertson, 1977)

Alcoholism, Kessel, Neil & Walton, Henry
(Penguin Books Ltd, 1965)

Allergy? Think About Food, Lewis, Susan
(Wisebuy Publications, 1984)

Aromatherapy for Women, Tisserand, Maggie
(Thorsons Ltd, 1985)

Chemical Victims, Mackarness, Richard
(Pan Books Ltd, 1976)

Fears and Phobias, Marks, Isaac M.
(William Heinemann Medical Books, London, 1969)

Gestalt Therapy, Perls, Frederick, Hefferline & Goodman
(Crown Publishers Inc., New York, 1951)

Living with Fear, Understanding and Coping with Anxiety,
Marks, Isaac M.
(McGraw-Hill Book Company, London & New York, 1978)

*Low Blood Sugar (Hypoglycaemia), The 20th Century
Epidemic?*, Budd, Martin L.
(Thorsons Publishers Ltd, 1984)

Not All In the Mind, Mackarness, Richard
(Pan Books Ltd, 1976)

Peace From Nervous Suffering, Weekes, Claire
(Angus & Robertson, 1972)

Phobias, Mitchell, Ross
(Pelican Books, 1982)

Phobias and Obsessions, Melville, Joy
(George Allen & Unwin, 1977)

Psychiatric Aspects of Minimal Brain Dysfunction in Adults,
Bellak, Leopold (ed.)
(Gene & Stratton, N.Y. & London, 1979)

Self Help For Your Nerves, Weekes, Claire
(Angus & Robertson, 1969)

The Myth of Neurosis, a Case for Moral Therapy, Wood, Garth
(Macmillan London Ltd, 1983)

The Tranquillizer Trap, Melville, Joy
(Fontana Paperbacks, 1984)

You and Neurosis, Eysenck, H. J.
(Maurice Temple Smith Ltd, 1977)

Useful Addresses

Anorexic Aid, The Priory Centre, 11 Priory Road, High Wycombe, Bucks.

Bach Flower Remedies, The Edward Bach Centre, Mount Vernon, Sotwell, Wallingford, Oxon OX10 0PZ

British Acupuncture Association, 34 Alderney Street, London SW1V 4EU
Register of practitioners on request.

British Homoeopathic Association, 27a Devonshire Street, London W1N 1RJ
The association has a list supplied by the Faculty of Homoeopathy of all the homoeopathic doctors and hospitals throughout the UK. They also run courses in first-aid and homoeopathy for the lay person.

British Hypnotherapy Association, 67 Upper Berkeley Street, London W1H 7DH
Send for list of practitioners.

British Society of Medical & Dental Hypnosis,
c/o Ms. M. Samuels, 42 Links Road, Ashtead, Surrey
The society keeps a list of members in various parts of the country who are willing to accept patients for treatment with hypnosis. Patients must be referred through their own doctor.

Churches Council for Health and Healing, Marylebone Road, London NW1 5LT

Harry Edwards Spiritual Healing Sanctuary, Burrows Lea, Shere, Guildford, Surrey

Institute for Neuro-Physiological Psychology, Warwick House, 4 Stanley Place, Chester, Cheshire

MIND (National Association for Mental Health), 22 Harley Street, London W1N 2ED
Will give advice and information.

National Federation of Spiritual Healers, Old Manor Farm Studio, Church Street, Sunbury-on-Thames, Middlesex TW16 6RG
(List of member healers in all parts of the country)

Phoenix Project, 4 Manorbrook, Blackheath, London SE3 9AW
Will advise those who suspect that they might have a drink problem.

Pre-Menstrual Tension Advisory Service, PO Box 268, Hove, Sussex BN3 1RW

Psychotherapy Centre, 67 Upper Berkeley Street, London W1N 2ED
Will recommend private psychotherapists.

Pyramid Healing, 'Mysteries', 9 Monmouth Street, London WC2

Relaxation for Living, 29 Burwood Park Road, Walton-on-Thames, Surrey
Send large sae for information about relaxation classes, correspondence courses, leaflets and books. There is also a cassette available called 'Self-help Relaxation', which can be obtained from the above address.

Samaritans, Local branches in telephone books, details in Citizens Advice Bureaux and libraries. For those who are feeling desperate.

Shiatsu Society, 11 Ivydene Road, Reading, Berks.
For all those interested in Shiatsu; it promotes communication

between involved individuals and provides information for the public.

Traditional Acupuncture Society, 11 Grange Park, Stratford-upon-Avon, Warwickshire CV37 6XH
Send sae for list of local members or £1 for list of members who use the letters MTAcS and do not advertise.

Yoga for Health Foundation, Ickwell Bury, Biggleswade, Beds. SG18 9EF

Cassettes
There are many Self-help cassettes now available, some just for relaxation and some specifically for agoraphobia:
Who's Afraid of Agoraphobia? Alice Neville.
Also cassettes produced individually. Send sae for details to the author.

Dr Claire Weekes' cassettes and records are available from 16 Rivermead Court, Ranelagh Gardens, London SW6 3RT

Lake Isle Relaxation
Tapes written and recorded by Peter Cauldwell, College of Surgeons graduate with 30 years' experience in relaxation techniques, anxiety and pain control. Send for details to Lake Isle Relaxation, 33 Oakfield Avenue, Wrenbury, Nantwich, Cheshire CW5 8ER
Also available: Lake Isle Relaxation Response Card; the monitor pad changes colour to indicate whether you are stressed, tense, calm or relaxed.

New World Cassettes, 113 Strawberry Vale, Twickenham, Middlesex TW1 4SJ
Illustrated free catalogue on request.

Relaxation cassettes and biofeedback instruments can be obtained from: *Aleph One Ltd*, The Old Courthouse, High Street, Bottisham, Cambridge CB5 9BA

General:
See *Here's Health* and *New Health* magazine advertisements for

biorhythm charts, biofeedback equipment, essential oils for aromatherapy, alternative medical practitioners etc.

Exercise Rebounders can be obtained from:
Wholistic Research Co. Ltd, Bright Haven, Robin's Lane, Lolworth, Cambridge CB3 8HH

Index